D0820850

# *A*
# PASSION
## *for*
# FASHION

*Achieving Your Fashion
Dreams One Thread
at a Time*

# NICK VERREOS
## with David Paul

**Post Hill Press**
275 Madison Avenue, 14th Floor
New York, NY 10016
posthillpress.com

Printed in the United States of America
1 2 3 4 5 6 7 8 9 10

# Contents

## CHAPTER 6

# Careers in Fashion: A Glossary

## CHAPTER 7

# Reality of the Fashion Business

## CHAPTER 8

# The Power and Pitfalls of Press

## CHAPTER 9

# Project Runway: Dish from the Runway, Workroom, and Beyond

## CHAPTER 10

# Threads of Advice

# FOREWORD

Nick Verreos and I first met at the auditions for *Project Runway* season two in March 2005. I was one of three members of the judging panel and Nick was among the 100+ designers that we were interviewing that day in Los Angeles. Although this was only season two, I was already weary from the cattle call and having an attack of ever-mounting frustration with uneven talent and lackluster presentation skills. Nick arrived as a potent antidote to the doldrums. He instantly enthralled us with fabulous concepts, superb execution, and a charismatic command of the room. It was a wow moment!

Since that fateful day, Nick and I have enjoyed eleven years of friendship. It's true that the fashion industry certainly unites us, but more important is our mutual love of teaching. Nick is the consummate teacher; it's in his DNA and earns him the greatest respect. Whether he's conducting a class at the prestigious Fashion Institute of Design and Merchandising, reporting from the red carpet, hosting a fashion event, or dressing a celebrity, Nick teaches. He brings depth of knowledge and experience, historical context, trend relevance, and, frankly, just plain common sense to all that he does. Listening to and observing Nick, I always feel better educated and informed.

*A Passion for Fashion* is a must-read for everyone who's contemplating entering the fashion industry in any capacity. Allow Nick to guide you through this daunting maze, deliver the hard-core realities, and dispel the pervasive myths. He serves as liege, éminence grise, and provocateur. As readers, absorb, synthesize, and relish the journey. You're in the hands of a master!

—*Tim Gunn*

# INTRODUCTION

# It's Show Time!

It was 7:56 a.m. on a Saturday morning when the sound of the door-bell echoed through my apartment. It was a shrill sound that I was not ready to hear on my day off. In a frazzled state, I made my way down the stairs, still wiping the sleep from my eyes and definitely not looking fashionable in any way, shape or form. I opened the door and standing before me was a tall beauty named Amara. She was at my door for one reason and one reason only: it was time to audition for *Project Runway*.

For weeks I had been mulling over a decision: whether or not to attend the casting of a relatively new reality competition show called *Project Runway*. Along with my partner, David Paul, I had launched my clothing line, NIKOLAKI, in 2001. Since then, we had been quite busy designing, draping, making patterns, cutting fabrics and fulfilling orders that were coming in from hundreds of stores across the country and internationally. I had also continued my side career as a freelance patternmaker. I was working out of my home, which doubled as my work studio, in order to pay the rent and fulfill all the orders that were arriving for my clothing line. If that wasn't enough, I also had a third side-career; an instructor at my alma mater, the Fashion Institute of Design & Merchandising (FIDM). So why would I even consider stopping all of that to be on a reality competition TV program? Call me crazy, but I was.

Along with many other viewers, I had watched the first season of *Project Runway*, which at the time was on the Bravo Network. As someone who was already working in the fashion industry, I had been quite skeptical of this new reality show which would crown a winner with the title of "America's Next Top Fashion Designer." You may remember—back in the early aughts—the reality show world was filled with MTV *Real World* hot tubs, Survivors eating bugs on an island, and a Bachelor picking amongst a bevy of beauties to find his perfect wife. So, when this little show came on the air and showed fashion designers actually creating garments from inception, I was mesmerized and thrilled to see the artistry and talent on display. I watched and immediately was hooked, but I never thought I could be one of those contestants. It wasn't until I received an email containing information on the castings for Season 2 that I started wondering if this might be an opportunity for me.

I know this may sound over the top, but the week prior to the casting was one of the most stressful weeks of my life. Little did I know that this was "kid's stuff" compared to what I would soon be dealing with on the show. You would think that just showing up to a TV show casting would be an easy decision, but it was not for me. It may come as a shock but I had never done TV prior to *Project Runway* and I was a bit frightened of even the thought of doing it. In addition, I was totally freaked out at the idea of showing up to the casting with a long line of hopeful designers, and standing alongside MY OWN students or former students from FIDM (Mon Dieu!). I had this recurring dream—or nightmare—of seeing some of my students standing in line, recognizing me and saying "Mr. Verreos, what are YOU doing here . . . Aren't you already a successful designer? You're our instructor for goodness sakes!" For some silly reason, I thought this would be embarrassing for me; this isn't something an established fashion designer and fashion school instructor should be doing.

And, of course, there were the obvious thoughts about being rejected. I was happy doing what I loved to do, and was content, but I knew there was more out there for me to achieve. I had been working hard at creating my own fashion label, but with every successful achievement, there were five setbacks that kept me from really reaching the potential I knew I was capable of. I half-jokingly would tell people that "When God was giving out the 'Good Luck' tickets, I must have been at the bar!"

I finally decided I was going to take on the challenge. I picked up the phone and called Amara to fill her in on my decision and feel her out about coming with me to the casting. There was nothing in the guidelines that stated anything about bringing a model, but I thought if I am going to do this, I'm going to do it 110%! I didn't have anything to offer her, except for maybe breakfast at Denny's after, but before I could finish asking, Amara said "When and Where? I'll be there!"

Flashback to that early Saturday morning and answering my door to Miss Amara, who was ready to help me take on my fashion dreams. She quickly slipped into a beautiful herringbone Edwardian sleeve jacket, silk harem pants, and a tie-neck blouse; all new pieces I had completed only days prior. We grabbed our coffee and were off to wait in line with hundreds of other hopeful designers.

Upon our arrival we dutifully signed up at the check-in desk and took our rightful place at the back of the line that seemed to stretch a full city block. No sooner did we get ourselves settled in for what we anticipated to be a LONG day in the hot LA sun, when a girl spotted Amara looking fabulous and quickly asked if she was a designer. Amara turned to me and said "No, this is the designer, Nick Verreos." With a wide eyed exclamation, the girl said "Mr. Verreos! It's me Nicole, your former student! What are you doing here?!" I remember thinking if there was an easy escape route, I would have been sprinting down the busy streets of Los Angeles. Timidly, I answered her with the obvious, that I was here to audition for the show.

Suddenly, I realized she was wearing a headset and quickly spoke into her mic, announcing to the powers that be that "I have Nick Verreos here and I'd like to take him to the holding room immediately." Quickly, the former student, that I was so worried would be my worst nightmare, unexpectedly became my savior. Within minutes we were ushered into a green room where Amara stripped naked and within seconds had changed into one of my bias cut silk gowns. She uttered, "I think this will be more impacting." Yes, it will, Amara, yes it will.

Soon I was standing in front of a panel of judges, including Tim Gunn, who after a few quick minutes uttered the words "You're in!"

# CHAPTER 1

# My Passion for Fashion

## From Missouri to Venezuela?

A lot of people are shocked when I tell them that I was born in St. Louis, Missouri. Somehow it doesn't seem fitting. People see me as being a bit more "international" or cosmopolitan as opposed to a . . . Midwesterner?! However, while I was born there, I could not really tell you anything about it. Only weeks after my birth, I was on a plane with my mom and *Mamaíta (Grandmother)* and flown to what was then the very sophisticated and exotic South American nation of Venezuela.

A little background might be needed here: My father, Jim, was also born in St. Louis. He is a first generation Greek-American whose father had left the homeland on a boat and ended up, like so many others, at Ellis Island. When he told the Customs officer his surname was Veriopulos, they instantly shortened it and wrote down "Verreos"; a very typical U.S. immigrant story. After attending St. Louis University School of Business Administration and Law School, my father ended up in Washington D.C. where he worked as an Attaché for the U.S. State Department. After years of traveling for work in Europe, Asia and Africa (can you imagine if they had frequent flyer programs back in the day?), he ended up in the Central American nation of Panama working as the Communications Attaché for the U.S. Embassy. This is where he met my mother.

Mr. Venezuela: fashionable at an early age.

My mother, Raquel, came from the very prominent Arias family. It's kind of a funny joke among Panamanians, that every other person claims to be related to the Arias family. However, my mother, in fact, did. Two of her great uncles, Arnulfo and Hermodio Arias, rose to the prominence of President of Panama. Arnulfo, in fact, was President six times (that's how it used to be back in Panama!). Her great cousin was Roberto Arias, Ambassador to the Court of St. James and husband to Dame Margot Fonteyn, the world-famous ballerina.

My parents soon married and moved to Mexico City where my dad continued his work at the U.S. Embassy. My mom was 9 months pregnant when he received transfer orders to go to Venezuela. As soon as he found out, he told my mom (along with her mother) to get to the U.S., so his son could be born in his hometown of St. Louis, Missouri. So, that's what happened in February of 1967. Soon after my birth—once it was safe to have a baby fly on a Pan Am Boeing 707 jet—my parents and I went to Caracas, Venezuela, where my father's new job awaited him.

# My First Fashion Muse

My earliest memory of having an interest in fashion began as a child in Venezuela. Because of my father's job at the U.S. Embassy, I vividly remember my mom getting ready for her many diplomatic functions. My parents would be attending an event at the Caracas Country Club or an Ambassador's residence, and without fail, there I was on the floor or dining room table, drawing my mom and her chiffon caftan dress, big bouffant 70s hairstyle and oversized turquoise earrings. The reason I know this is because my mom (bless her heart!) kept every single sketch and therefore I have the proof—down to the bouffant and J.Lo-before-J.Lo earrings. I drew my dad also, but his sketch would be of a very skinny man in a tuxedo and black bow tie: BORING. My mother would recall that they would return from their parties and I would be asleep next to my stack of fashion sketches.

Drawing was my way of talking. I woke up and drew and then went to bed drawing. And while I sketched typical things young kids my age would draw—airplanes, houses, trees, etc.—somehow, I always returned to drawing women and their fashion.

Embassy Chic: my parents attending a diplomatic function.

# Stewardess Style: Fashion Muse No. 2

My love of drawing women and their style got very interesting in that early part of childhood when we began traveling. My mom worked for Hilton Hotels and besides the fact that my father was a diplomat, we also got to travel because of her hotel connections. Summer holidays were spent in the Venezuelan resort island of Margarita, as well as traveling to the Netherlands Antilles islands of Aruba and Curacao. During this entire time, I became obsessed with flight attendants and naturally, their uniforms.

I am sure that many of you right now are thinking "flight attendants?" When we think of flight attendants now, fashionable muses do not always come to mind. One mainly thinks of a not-so-polite person barking orders to put your carry-on in the overhead or to turn off your electronic device. But during my adolescence in the early 1970s, flight attendants were fabulous! They were chic and stylish in their Pucci or Adolfo ensembles and were more fashion-forward than utilitarian. To me, they were my first "supermodels." Besides my mom, flight attendants—or stewardesses as they were called back then—became my second "Fashion Muses." I loved sketching them and their outfits.

While other kids my age were probably playing soccer or baseball, I would pass the time after school drawing "Airlines of the World" stewardess fashion. I would get a list of every country in the world from my second grade geography book and then draw the uniform for a flight attendant from countries across the globe. Naturally, these weren't just suits with white blouses. My version of an Air India flight attendant, for example, involved a fabulous Sari that would somehow zip-off into a hot-shorts ensemble during an emergency landing. Every stewardess had an over-the-top hat and I even made up a "Nick Verreos" logo for the print of the scarves.

# A Foreign Land

After many happy years in Venezuela, my parents decided that it was time to move to the United States and specifically the San Francisco

Ready for take-off: my childhood sketches of stewardess divas.

Bay Area. My father's brother and his family lived there and there-fore, my dad felt it was time for us to join his family. I did not speak a word of English and there I was, in San Bruno—about 20 miles south of San Francisco—a lost fashion-loving kid. Even though I had been born in the United States, I felt like a complete foreigner, since for all intents and purposes, I was. There were no other "Hispanic" kids that I knew of and certainly no one else in my school who spoke Spanish, the only language I knew. The situation wasn't any better with the Greek community in San Francisco. My father tried to get us acquainted with our Greek heritage and attend the city's Greek Orthodox church but that was a fail, since neither my sister nor I spoke any Greek and therefore we did not understand a single word of anything being said. Feeling like a foreigner in my own country, I retreated to my happy place, creating my own wonderful world of fashion by drawing, and drawing a lot.

# Pageant Mania

I had now moved away from sketching my mom (no more fabulous diplomatic parties, certainly not in San Bruno, California), and I had also grown bored of my "fantasy" flight attendants. I discovered two things: beauty pageants and fashion magazines.

After moving to the U.S. and feeling like a foreigner in a strange land, naturally, I began having feelings of nostalgia for what I considered my home: Venezuela. It was to my delight when one night in 1979 the *Miss Universe* beauty pageant aired on television. I was FASCINATED. I could not take my eyes off of the TV screen. I was especially transfixed by the national costumes parade of nations with beautiful women from all over the world. It was like my "Stewardesses of the World" fantasy sketches come to life! And did I mention THE GOWNS? How could I resist all those sequins and iridescent taffeta? What also excited me was that the contestant from Venezuela had made the top ten. Her name was Maritza Sayalero and she was tall, gorgeous and chic, complete with a top-knot chignon. The fact that this beauty from my former "home" had made the Miss Universe finals had me acting as if I was watching the Superbowl and my team was winning. In fact, my entire family was going berserk.

*Señorita Muy Bonita!* My sketch of a Miss Venezuela.

There was just one little problem; the very evening of the Miss Universe pageant, my parents were sending both my sister and I on a red-eye flight to Miami to spend the summer with my aunt. The flight departed at midnight and we had to leave my house at 10 p.m. and therefore, we were not able to watch the final part of the pageant. I was so mad that I would not be able to watch the entire show. If it wasn't for the fact that I loved airplanes and more importantly, seeing flight attendants, I would have probably proceeded to conjure up the worse temper tantrum a 12-year-old could muster.

I spent the flight drawing and I'm sure my sketchpad from that night was filled with pageant gowns, crowns and sashes. The minute we landed and my aunt was there at the gate to greet us, instead of *"Hola Tia!"* (Hello aunt!), I shouted to her: "Who won?" Answer: MISS VENEZUELA! It was the first time a Miss Venezuela had won the Miss Universe pageant. I can now identify that specific instance in 1979 as the moment I had my new muse: Miss Venezuela.

I watched the pageants not to gawk at pretty girls in scantily-clad swimwear but instead to see the national costumes and more importantly, the gowns. It was always about the fashion. This was heightened during the early 80s when the "Miss Venezuela" pageant became known as a huge "TV fashion show" and highlighted some of the most beautiful women in the world.

Every year, on the day the "Miss Venezuela" pageant would air, I would be on the floor of our living room in front of the TV with my sketch pad in hand. The show would feature gowns from all the top couturiers of Caracas, including Paris-trained Guy Meliet, and designs from Gianfranco Ferre for Christian Dior Haute Couture. I kid you not when I say that there was no better once-a-year fashion show on TV than the "Miss Venezuela" pageant.

## Hide the Vogue

During those awkward teenage years, I also discovered fashion magazines. I would tag along with my mom on her weekly trips to the local Safeway and head straight to the magazine stand. I would look to my right, then to my left, to make sure no one was looking. And then I would quickly grab a *Vogue* magazine and stuff it in a *Sports Illustrated* or something non-fashion. I didn't want anyone wondering why a young 14-year-old boy was looking at a woman's fashion magazine. Saying that now, it sounds utterly ridiculous. At the time, I had enough things to deal with, the last one being made fun of as a "sissy" who loves fashion magazines.

My mom, of course, knew that I loved fashion magazines, bless her heart. She fed my passion for fashion with an endless supply. I would take them home every month as if they were Christmas gifts. I would then run to my room, plop myself on the bed, and look at the photos, the fashion ads and the models, and engulf myself in my own little world. I would also take my sketch notebook which I always had with me and draw. I would draw the fashions in the magazines and also be inspired to draw my own designs. Eventually, I began to sketch fantasy collections; 30 looks, including, of course, the final wedding gown. Somehow I knew that every designer, at the time, always ended their fashion shows with a wedding gown. At least they did back then.

I am sure I wasn't the first fashion-loving teenager who has been inspired by *Vogue* or *Elle* and obviously not the last. Nevertheless, I am most indebted to those magazines for igniting my passion and more importantly, for having a mom who not just supported it but enabled it, thank goodness!

# High School Hobby

My Passion for Fashion only intensified throughout my adolescence and into my high school years. Every day, after school, I couldn't wait to get home and start drawing and reading the many fashion magazines my mother now bought me to help quench my insatiable desire for fashion. I began to seek out any resource available that involved fashion. Obviously, there was no hiding my excitement when Elsa Klensch came on CNN or Jeanne Beker was reporting on all the exotic fashion week events on Fashion TV. I would become lost in this new beautiful fantasy world.

But then something happened: Senior year in high school. I was forced to think about my future and what I was going to do with my life. I needed to decide where I wanted to continue my studies and all those nerve-racking decisions a 17-year-old is supposed to consider. I remember thinking that I had no real desire to do anything but draw fashion, but at the same time, I never considered enrolling in a fashion college. It just didn't seem like an option, especially for a young man. I remember having my requisite counselor visit to talk about college and my post-high school thoughts. I asked my counselor if there were any colleges that he knew of that had majors in Fashion Illustration or something similar. I will never forget how quickly he rebuffed my thoughts and in fact said "there are no jobs in that!"

# Fashion School Not

Following that meeting, I did do some investigating on my own and discovered that indeed there were many higher institutions that offered programs in Fashion and Design. But as all my fellow students were boasting about going to Stanford, Berkley, and such esteemed universities, I was almost embarrassed to say that I wanted to attend fashion school; it didn't seem like "real college." Looking back at this, I can't believe how I had become so self-loathing of my secret hobby. No one made me think that the possibility of attending Fashion or Art school was a lesser option, especially not my parents. I think I just came up with this conclusion on my own for whatever silly and unsubstantiated reason.

# A Fashionable Diplomat?

In absence of not being comfortable with attending fashion school, I had to come up with something else that sounded remotely interesting to me. More importantly, that path needed to mirror a more "traditional" college route. Are you ready for what I decided on? Political science and international relations. Yes, you read that right. My dad was a diplomat so I thought why can't I follow in his footsteps and also be a diplomat? At the very least, I would be a very fashionable one, I thought. I was bilingual, grew up abroad, and loved traveling (Hello flight attendant uniforms!). I therefore applied to the University of California, Berkley as well as U.C.L.A. and lo and behold, I was accepted. Well, that was easy! After visiting the serenely gorgeous UCLA campus in Westwood and its surrounding Bel Air neighborhood, I naturally decided to leave the fog of the Bay Area and head to sunny Southern California. My decision was made and I was ready to embark on a new life devoted to International Relations.

Guess what I did the entire time I was at UCLA? Yes, I sketched. I continued to be diligent in my classes, writing thesis' on the "Conflict between Eritrea and Ethiopia" and "Soviet Union in Afghanistan" and even interned with a renowned government agency. However, if you took a look at my notes in all those Political Science classes, the edges would be filled with evening gowns and fabulous sketches of models in Haute Couture. My college mates would every now and then nudge me and ask (quietly) "Why in the name of God are YOU studying Political Science? You should be a Fashion Designer!" I would just disregard their comments and say, "Oh, I like to sketch . . . leave me alone."

My entire dorm room wall was covered in fashion magazine ads of Linda Evangelista, Naomi Campbell, and Christy Turlington in Versace. There would be glossy photos of Claudia Schiffer in Chanel suits, and *Vogue* magazine covers of Isabella Rossellini and Nastassja Kinski. My roommate was a Computer Engineering student, and you can only imagine what he thought living inside my fashion fantasy world. Also, this display did not help curb the comments of my doubting friends at UCLA. They continued to press me on why I wasn't studying fashion design.

## Do 1 Really Want to Be a Diplomat?

As graduation time approached, I began having those "tummy feelings." Did I really want to have a career as a diplomat? Did I want to go through the trials and tribulations of taking the Foreign Service Exam, or moving to Washington D.C. . . . or Madagascar? The more I thought about it, the more I was convinced to follow my love: fashion. It would take me awhile—4+ years in college—but I finally came out of the closet, as it were. I graduated from UCLA with a B.A. in Political Science/International Relations but during the months following my graduation, without telling my parents, I secretly applied to all the top design schools—Parsons, FIT, and FIDM. This would be a test. My family always said I had a natural talent and that I was an exceptional sketch artist, but I wanted to hear it from actual design professionals. It's one thing if your mom and dad think you're good, they are your parents and they love you unconditionally. However, it's another story if experts in the field actually say that you are talented. It's like those parents on "American Idol" who say "my daughter can SING!" while you're watching and thinking "Nope! She's tone deaf!"

To my surprise, I was accepted to every design school to which I applied. I eventually decided to attend FIDM after being invited to attend their "Debut" Fashion Show, a runway extravaganza that features the collections of the college's ten Advanced Fashion Design students. These students were considered the crème de la crème of the school. After seeing the show, I was determined to be one of those students showing my "Nick Verreos" collection whenever it was time for my FIDM Debut.

Now, all I had to do was break the news to my parents. I knew my mom would be ecstatic but it was my father that I was worried about. What would a stern man of Greek descent think of his one-and-only son, attending FASHION SCHOOL. He almost cried when I told him. He couldn't hold his emotions, describing how he had been waiting so long to hear this! He then confessed to me how he had always wanted to study art and be an artist himself. To my surprise, he was thrilled that I could now "live my dream." Only then did I recall, when I was very young back in Caracas, my dad would sketch the most beautiful drawings. He would illustrate the most elaborate airplanes, the most exquisite houses, and draw beautiful faces. I soon realized that it had all come full circle, my dad had passed on his "artistic gene."

I had an amazing time at FIDM but it was also very, very difficult. The workload surprised me. It's a fashion college after all, how could it be difficult, I naively thought! But I LOVED it. I was being challenged and I challenged myself. I was finally, after all these years, in my element and this was where I belonged. It took me a while to get there, but the important part is I got there. I wanted to tell my story, to show that I didn't get to fashion school immediately; it took me some time and some "growing up" to realize that this, indeed, was my path. Some people know right away what they want from life and some do not. I was in the latter group, but no matter what your path, the best way forward is to keep moving and reach for your dreams.

# CHAPTER 2

# Preparing for Fashion School

## Fashion School History

Going to fashion school or attending a college to study Fashion has never been as popular as it has been in recent years. But, if you look back only 30 or 40 years ago, this was not the case. The history of a fashion school probably began with basic trade courses or high school courses most commonly called "Home Economics." In fact, I remember having to take Home Economics back when I was in middle school, getting the basics of cooking, laundry and for the first time, turning on a sewing machine.

At the turn of the 20th Century, home economics was a critical pathway for American women, in particular; it became an avenue for higher education, or at least a way to receive "preparatory" instructions on how to properly run a house, cook and yes, even sew. Sewing and pattern-making were considered more of a woman's job. But interestingly enough, in terms of Fashion Design, it is a man's name, Charles Frederick Worth, that is most associated with being the first Couturier and having his label sewn into a garment and claim it as his own design.

The French (naturally) set up one of the first schools solely devoted to the art, business, and technical trade of fashion back in 1927 with their school: Chambre Syndicale de Couture Parisienne. However, the universality of fashion schools is something of a modern development. Its popularity became more and more prevalent as fashion became mainstream and accessible to everyone. This has only increased with the advent of the Internet and social media. The availability of fashion and the process of fashion design is now a normal part of our modern vernacular.

# The Cool Thing to Do

Now, in our modern times, it seems that everyone and their mother wants to be in the fashion business. It has become a much sought-after profession and industry to be part of. Fashion Designers can now come out of hiding and step in front of the gilded silk curtains, becoming international superstars and multimillion dollar brands. The mass democratization of fashion and worldwide reach of the Red Carpet in the last decade has also had a huge impact on young people wanting to "get in on the action." And of course, I would be remiss not to mention shows such as *Project Runway* which have definitely played a very important role in getting people interested in the world of fashion and all its glamorous byproducts. Nonetheless, I am constantly reminding anyone that will listen, that the fashion world is a very tough business. With all its beauty and excitement, there is a ton of hard work and risk. You need to go into this profession with your eyes wide open and not be clouded by all the pomp and circumstance.

# Why Fashion School?

OK, now it's time to delve into the Big Question: Why attend a fashion school? This is a question that I get asked a lot. Many people take pride in being self-taught; it's almost like a badge of honor. I can definitely understand why you would be proud of this achievement. I can only imagine how hard it would be to tackle a career as difficult as fashion design with little-to-no guidance. However, as wonderful as it might be to start out as a self-taught designer, I think it is still necessary to study Fashion Design in a structured environment and get a degree. There are many reasons I can state, but the most obvious one is that it helps you get a job. Most design companies, whether they are small or large, require a fashion degree for just an entry-level position.

Secondly, nothing can truly substitute for formal training by professional teachers in all the major disciplines. Fashion programs are structured to maximize your potential and give you a well-rounded education in sketching, proper fashion sewing, draping, pattern-making, costing, merchandising, creating presentation/inspiration boards, and designing collections. All these facets of becoming a complete fashion designer require actual schooling. Most importantly, I think that it is vital to be in an environment of design. When you are surrounded by talented people and allow yourself to be immersed in the process of design, you can truly flourish and reach your greatest potential. And ultimately, it allows you to meet like-minded artists and collaborate. Networking and creating relationships with fellow students will guide you and help you succeed in the vast world of fashion.

# Nick Tips

Now that I've laid out reasons why you should attend a fashion college, it's time I give you some of my "Nick Tips" to help you prepare and subsequently, get the most out of attending.

## Do Your Fashion School Homework

Before deciding on what school to attend, do your homework. Research the Who, What, Where and Why of all the top fashion schools. Obviously, New York and Los Angeles are the most geographically fashion-centric cities in the United States. However, there are other areas that are power-houses of fashion and have amazing opportunities for schooling and work. Orange County, CA wouldn't necessarily be thought of as a fash-ion capital, but it is widely regarded as the top city for Action Sportswear and Surfwear. Portland and Seattle are both considered leading cities for Activewear, with amazing companies like Nike, REI and Columbia

Sportswear. In addition, many of the top design schools aren't just located in N.Y.C. or L.A. You'll find the highly regarded Savannah College of Art and Design (SCAD) in Savannah, Georgia as well as Rhode Island School of Design (RISD), located in Providence, Rhode Island.

If you're interested in studying abroad, there are many fantastic schools to choose from. It's a much more expensive alternative, but if you are able to afford it, there are many options that will offer an immense opportunity for higher education and personal growth. Examples of top fashion schools abroad include Central Saint Martins in London; Bunka Fashion College in Tokyo; Royal Academy of Fine Arts in Antwerp, Belgium; and Ecole de la Chambre Syndicale in Paris. Also, there are many U.S. fashion schools that offer programs that allow you to study abroad for a quarter, semester, or even a year.

Wherever you decide to attend school, it's important to understand that upon graduating and searching for employment, the highest percentage of jobs are still located in Los Angeles or on the East Coast. Los Angeles is, in fact, the highest employer of fashion and fashion manufacturing jobs in the nation, not New York City, as people may think. With that said, there are opportunities across the country for amazing jobs in the fashion industry.

From San Francisco to Chicago, to Miami and Texas, if you are prepared and excited for a career in fashion, you will find employment in a variety of places. I chose to stay in Los Angeles when deciding where to attend fashion school for two main reasons: First, I was instantly attracted to the Fashion Institute of Design & Merchandising and what the college had to offer me. Secondly, I had already created "roots" in L.A. after living here for several years while attending UCLA and it was starting to feel like home.

## Don't Feel Like You Need to Know Everything

In terms of preparing to attend a fashion school, don't feel intimidated if you do not know everything about fashion. Attending college is a big step in someone's life, so there will already be an immense amount of pressure to begin with. Nobody expects for you to arrive on campus being a fashion genius. Basic applications to top art schools and fashion colleges around the country require a portfolio, letters of recommendation, and an essay perhaps. They do not require you to have a ten-piece collection painstakingly created as part of your entrance exam. Because of my drawing skills, I was able to put together a rather impressive portfolio, but trust me when I say that I was sufficiently lacking in other disciplines.

On my first day of sewing class at FIDM, I was filled with nerves; I had never been so anxious in my life. I had a secret and I thought I was about to be exposed: I didn't really know how to sew. I also assumed that all my fellow students already had this talent and were sewing experts. Somehow I assumed that it was 1950 and every young girl got taught how to sew by their doting, chocolate chip-cookie making, stay-at-home mother. (What a generalization, right?) Well, imagine my surprise when the class began and 95% of my classmates were as clueless about the art of sewing as I was. In other words, don't feel as if you need to know everything. I often find that the people that act as if they know the most, usually end up knowing nothing!

## Buy a Sewing Machine

With that being said, before attending a fashion school, it's not a bad idea to start getting acquainted with a sewing machine and how to use one, especially if you have no idea how to sew. Once I was accepted to FIDM, I had my mom give me her Singer sewing machine we had back at our home tucked away in a closet. Now, to be honest, I didn't take it out of its case until I started my classes but at least I was ready and prepared!

Your college will most likely have industrial sewing machines, so you won't be getting a "heads up" on that skill, but trust me when I tell you that you will have plenty of homework to do on your home sewing machine. Sewing manufacturers such as Singer, Brother, and Viking all make great basic machines that are appropriate for someone beginning their journey.

I am always impressed when I meet 15 and 16-year-olds at events wearing designs that they've made and sewn themselves. These kids are already WAY ahead of where I was back at that age! So, while you don't need to be an expert or have an encyclopedic knowledge of fashion, it never hurts to get a jump start on your passion.

# CHAPTER 3

# Fundamentals of Sketching

## Sketching Tips & Tricks

There are many young people who want to go to fashion school who have amazing and unique design ideas but their sketching ability isn't as fab. What is my advice to those people? One word: croquis.

## What Is a Croquis?

Croquis derives from the French word *croquer*, which means to sketch quickly. In the fashion industry, a croquis is also a non-clothed drawing of a figure, usually standing straight and facing front, proportionally divided into 9 "heads."

In fashion design, we use a croquis as a template upon which we apply our designs. Think of it as a "paper doll," the kind kids would use to play with back in the day. There are several types of croquis—one for Flat/Technical Sketches and one for Fashion Sketches/Illustrations. *(Figure 3-1)*

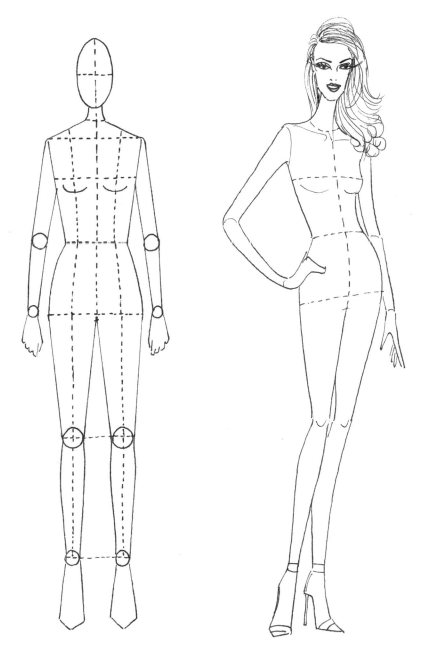

**Figure 3-1:** Technical Croquis and Fashion Croquis

# What Is a 9-Head Croquis?

A 9-head croquis is a figure divided into nine even sections. Each section the size of a "head" (the oval-shaped face of the model/figure). Usually on an 8 ½" × 11" piece of paper, a "head" measures out to be about 1¹/₁₆"—or just slightly more than an inch.

A "normal" (non-fashion style) human figure measures to approximately 8 heads, but in fashion sketching, we exaggerate the figure to make it more stylized. In fashion illustration, the legs and neck are usually more elongated, to create a longer silhouette. If you are doing a Costume Sketch or striving for something more realistic, then an 8 head figure is the best approach.

# How to Create Your Own 9-Head Croquis

On an 8 ½" × 11" piece of paper, use a ruler and lightly draw a vertical line down the center of the paper. Now, divide the line into nine equal parts. Like I stated above, you can make marks at 1¹/₁₆" apart:

1 = HEAD
1 ½ = SHOULDER
2 = BUST OR APEX
3 = NATURAL WAIST/ELBOW
3 ¼ = LOW WAIST
4 = HIPS/WRIST
4 ¼ = CROTCH
5 = MID-THIGH
6 = KNEE
7 = CALF
8 = ANKLE
9 = BOTTOM OF FEET *(Figure 3-2)*

When it comes to the rest of the body of the croquis, there are sections that are also divided to help make the illustration visually balanced. For example, we use a 1½ head measurement for the shoulders as well as the hips. In other words, the shoulders are the same width as the hips on a fashion croquis. *(Figure 3-3)*

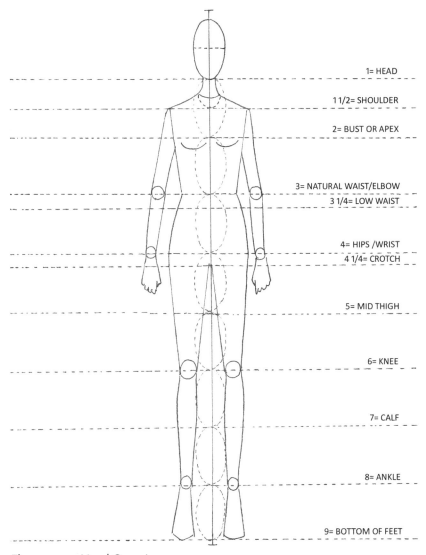

1= HEAD

1 1/2= SHOULDER

2= BUST OR APEX

3= NATURAL WAIST/ELBOW

3 1/4= LOW WAIST

4= HIPS /WRIST

4 1/4= CROTCH

5= MID THIGH

6= KNEE

7= CALF

8= ANKLE

9= BOTTOM OF FEET

**Figure 3-2:** 9-Head Croquis

Now that you have made your own Flat Sketch croquis using my instructions, I would suggest outlining the croquis in a black marker. You can use this to slip under your blank drawing paper and whenever you want to draw a garment, it will always be proportionate! No longer will your knee-length skirt be too long or too short. A floor length

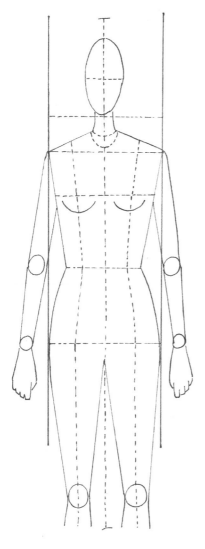

**Figure 3-3:** A Balanced Croquis (Shoulder equals Hips)

gown will actually be . . . floor length. And if you ever want to draw a plunging neckline, by using the croquis, you will be guaranteed to never have a too-revealing moment!

The basic croquis I have described and sketched are perfect when drawing the "Flat" or Technical Sketches I talked about, but they can also be used for basic one-dimensional fashion illustrations. Again, just think of them as if you were dressing those paper dolls when you were younger. (I did!)

# What Is a Flat Sketch?

So you might be asking yourself, what is a flat sketch? Flat sketches are drawings of clothing as if they are lying flat on a table or hanging perfectly on a hanger. Another term for Flat Sketch is a Technical Sketch. Both can be used interchangeably. Usually, a Technical Sketch will be a Flat Sketch but with the addition of construction information alongside the sketch. *(Figure 3-4)*

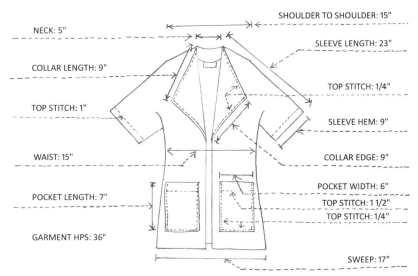

SHOULDER TO SHOULDER: 15"
NECK: 5"
SLEEVE LENGTH: 23"
COLLAR LENGTH: 9"
TOP STITCH: 1/4"
TOP STITCH: 1"
SLEEVE HEM: 9"
WAIST: 15"
COLLAR EDGE: 9"
POCKET WIDTH: 6"
POCKET LENGTH: 7"
TOP STITCH: 1 1/2"
TOP STITCH: 1/4"
GARMENT HPS: 36"
SWEEP: 17"

**Figure 3-4:** Flat Sketch vs. Technical Sketch

# What Is a Fashion Sketch Croquis?

A fashion sketch croquis involves a more stylized—or posed—figure. So, instead of a "flat" one-dimensional sketch, a fashion croquis is a complete figure that is slightly posed with movement. *(Figure 3-5)*

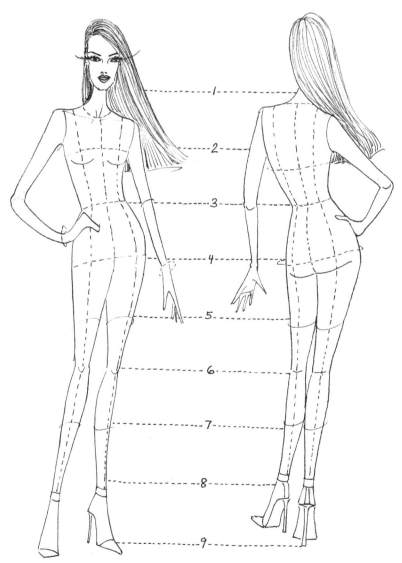

**Figure 3-5:** Fashion Sketch Croquis

Here are some examples of fashion sketch croquis. What I've done here is transfer the same rules of the basic croquis but made them into different fashion sketch poses. You are still using the concept of the 9-head croquis but instead of the figure looking "flat," your croquis is now much more stylized and shows more dimension. The following are some different fashion poses. Feel free to use them and GET SKETCHING! The more you practice, the better you will become and soon you won't need to use a croquis at all! *(Figures 3-6, 3-7, 3-8)*

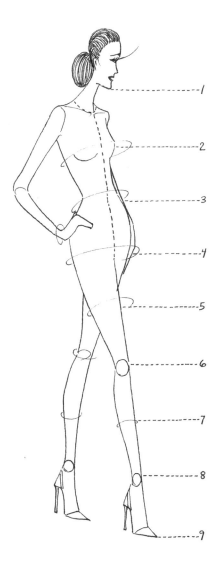

**Figures 3-6:** Fashion Sketch Croquis

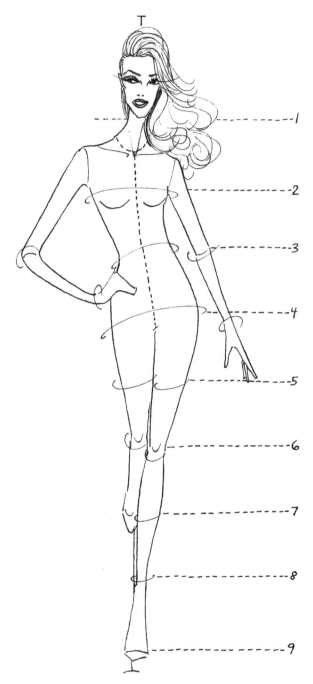

**Figure 3-7:** Fashion Sketch Croquis

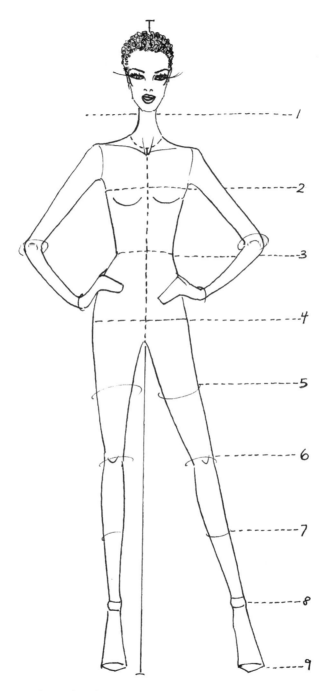

1

2

3

4

5

6

7

8

9

**Figure 3-8:** Fashion Sketch Croquis

# Nick Tips

Now that you have the croquis, it is time to get started on perfecting you drawing skills and creating more professional looking garments. In my many years of drawing fashion and instructing students on how to sketch, I've amassed some "Nick Tips" to help the amateur artist advance their skills.

Whether you are just beginning or have been drawing for a while, I am positive you will find some helpful information in the following pages. Many times, I taught students who were already very good artists, but after taking my class they would always come back to me saying just how much they had learned. This is exactly how I felt when I took my first Fashion Illustration class. I thought I "knew it all" and boy, was I wrong. My instructor taught me so much and I want to pass that on to the next generation of fashion illustrators and designers.

I realize that many flat and technical sketches are now done by computer and using computer programs, but there is still a lot of sketching done by hand. I think it is necessary to at least know the basics and I feel that by learning some of these tips, you will be that much better when using that computer program.

Before you begin any of these sketching "assignments," you will need the following:

1. Clean piece of paper.
2. Your croquis (to slip under the paper).
3. Pencil: I prefer a No. 2, or mechanical pencils with .7 mm lead.
4. Eraser.
5. Straight ruler: preferably, a clear ruler that you can see through but still has all the measurements.
6. Curved ruler such as a "French Curve" style.

***Are you ready to get started? Let's get drawing!***

# Drawing Collars

I want to start out this section with my lessons on drawing collars. Most everyone knows what a collar looks like, but when it comes to drawing them, it can get a bit complicated. There are a variety of collar styles from the basic shirt collar to the more complicated notched jacket lapel. I have specific "Nick Tricks" that are surefire ways of drawing a perfect collar EVERY TIME. Let's begin with the basic shirt collar:

## Shirt Collar

A standard shirt collar can also be described, in more fancy fashion terminology, as a Convertible Collar. I have a Four-Step Process for drawing this collar. *(Figure 3-9A)*

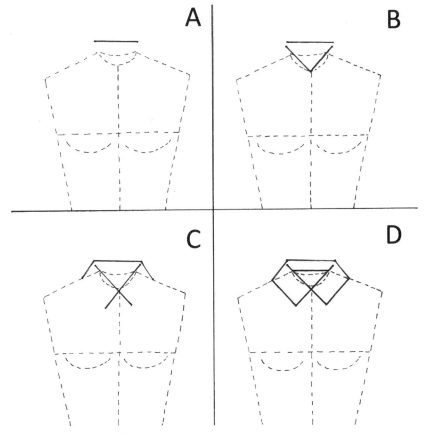

**Figure 3-9A:** Shirt Collar

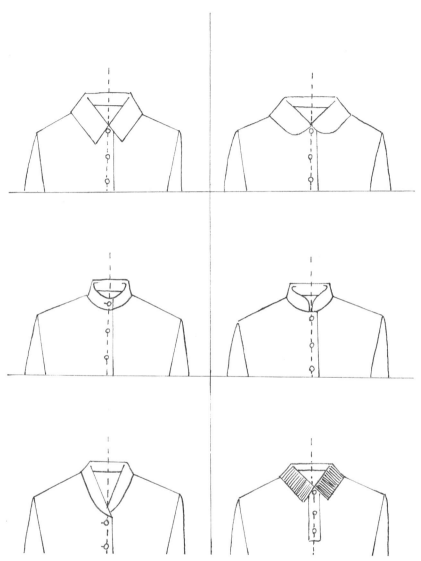

**Figure 3-9B:** Various Shirt Collar Styles

Begin with the croquis I've provided in Figure 3-2 and, if possible, enlarge the torso so you can practice this lesson several times. Slip the croquis under a clean piece of paper and follow these steps below:

1. Draw a straight line above the neck as seen here. I call this the "halo" (A).

2. Draw a "V", making sure that the point of the "V" touches the center front (CF) of the neck in your croquis and the top points of the "V" barely touch the "halo" line (B).
3. Draw diagonal lines that are parallel to each other. The top lines should touch the shoulder of your croquis. These lines should be equal in length. Repeat this step for the other side (C). These are the Collar Stand lines.
4. Connect these two lines and finally, draw a line slightly below the "halo" above the neck area of your croquis (D).

## Notched Lapel

A notched lapel is a collar usually seen in tailored garments such as jackets or coats. The notch of the collar is an "opening" seen on the seams where the proper collar and lapel portion of the jacket join. This opening varies in width depending on the design and style of the collar, lapel and garment. *(Figure 3-10)*

Drawing a notched lapel is a little more difficult than drawing a basic collar but only because it requires a few extra steps. Here is my foolproof Nine Step Guide to drawing a Single Breasted Notched Lapel:

1. Draw a straight line above the neck of your croquis. This is the same as the "halo" you drew for your regular shirt collar (A).
2. Next, draw an exaggerated "X." Notice how the "X" is not even, but has longer lines at the top and shorter lines at the bottom. In addition, make sure the point where your "X" crosses is on the center front (CF) line of your croquis and extends just a little bit beyond the center front. This is now the front of your jacket. Many people think that when you close your jacket, the edge of your garment is right at the center front but in fact, it is not, it's usually anywhere from ¼" to an inch or more beyond it (depending on the size of the buttons or style of jacket). (B)
3. Draw vertical lines down from the bottom of the "X." (C)
4. Draw diagonal lines (just like you did for the shirt collar), that touch your "halo" line with the shoulder of your croquis. These represent the collar stand. (D)
5. Draw two lines slightly below the collar stand that are parallel in direction to those lines. These lines should also be about the same length. Mark the halfway points of these lines (E).

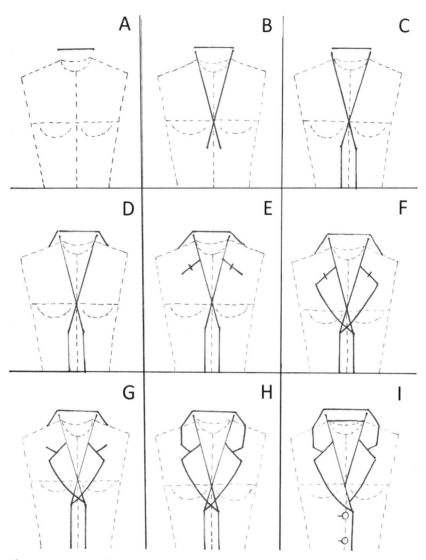

**Figure 3-10A:** Notched Lapel

6. Connect these lines with the lower points of your "X" with a slightly curved line. These should slightly resemble chopping knives (F). You have now drawn your lapels. Congratulations! But you are not done yet.

7. Now, go back to the halfway marks and draw short lines that slope upwards to create what looks like a sideways "V." (G)

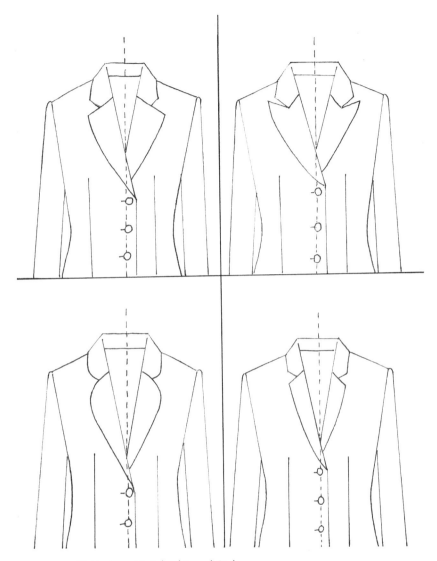

**Figure 3-10B:** Various Notched Lapel Styles

8. Connect the end point of these lines to the collar stand (H). This completes the collar portion of your notched lapel.

9. Lastly, draw a straight line to create the inside of your collar and go back to where your "knives" (lapels) cross and erase the lines as seen in (I).

## Double Breasted Collar

The rules for drawing a Double Breasted Collar are very similar to that of a Single Breasted Notched Lapel. It's the same nine steps, however, the only difference is in Step 2. When you draw an "X" for the Double Breasted Jacket, make it symmetrical with the lower points of that "X" ending up around the Princess Seam line of your croquis (B). From there, follow the same steps as the single breasted jacket and you will have your completed double breasted collar. *(Figure 3-11)*

**Figure 3-11:** Double Breasted Collar

## Peter Pan Collar

A "Peter Pan" style collar is usually a rounded collar, predominantly—but not exclusively—seen in children's clothes, but also popular for coats. It derives its name from the costume worn by Maude Adams in 1905 when she played Peter Pan, but I am sure this collar can trace its provenance to even earlier times and possibly traditional European folk-loric costumes. The steps to drawing a Peter Pan collar are basically the same as drawing a regular shirt collar but with a couple of differences, including the rounding out of the front edges. *(Figure 3-12A)*

1. Draw a straight line—the "Halo"—above the neck (A). This should be closer to the neckline of your croquis then when drawing the regular shirt collar.
2. Draw a "V," making sure that the point of the "V" touches the center front (CF) of your croquis and the top lines of the "V" barely touch the "halo" line (B).
3. Draw diagonal lines that connect the "halo" line to the shoulder part of your croquis (C). This is your collar stand.
4. Draw a curved line beginning from the Center Front (CF) that then connects with the diagonal lines you drew in Step 3 (D). Finally, draw a line slightly below the "halo" at the back neck area of your croquis (E).

# Drawing Shirts

Shirts come in many variations and styles. It is important that you learn the basics of drawing shirts and more importantly, different types of shirts. In Figure 3-12B I have shown you the right and wrong way to draw-ing a proper shirt. Pay special attention that you do not make the shirt too fitted or close to the body of your croquis. Also, watch out for the length. A lot of beginners make the mistake of drawing their shirts too short. Think about a dress shirt and where they end on you—whether you are a male or female. Normally, an average shirt ends around hip level or slightly below. So once again, utilize your valuable croquis for making sure the proportions are correct.

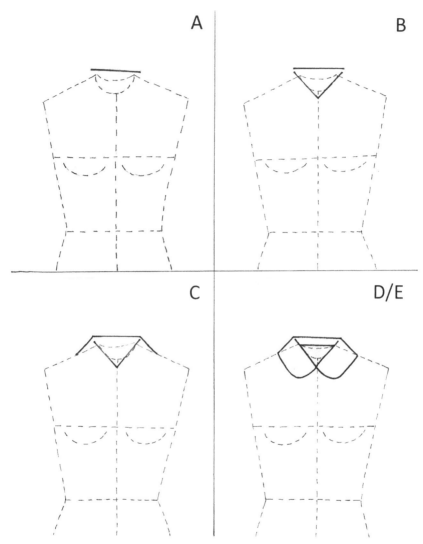

**Figure 3-12A:** Peter Pan Collar

# Fitted Shirt

See Figure 3-13.

1. Draw the shirt collar according to my "5 Steps to Draw a Collar" in Figure 3-9.
2. Draw the shoulders by just following the shoulder line in your croquis (A).

DO    DON'T

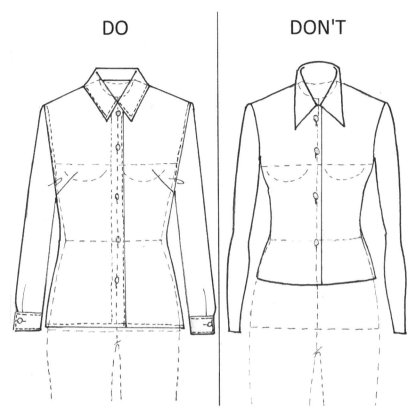

**Figure 3-12B:** Right and Wrong Way to Draw a Shirt

3. Next, draw the sides of your shirt by drawing a line beginning at the shoulder edge and ending around hip level. (B) This line will start out straight but will curve slightly at the waist and be slightly away from the croquis' body.

4. Connect the sides of the shirt with a straight line at the hip area to create the hem (C).

5. Draw the sleeves with straight lines, once again making sure to be slightly away from the croquis' arms (D).

6. Finish it off by drawing buttons and darts if applicable (E). *See the section on Drawing Shirt and Tops Details for how to draw buttons.*

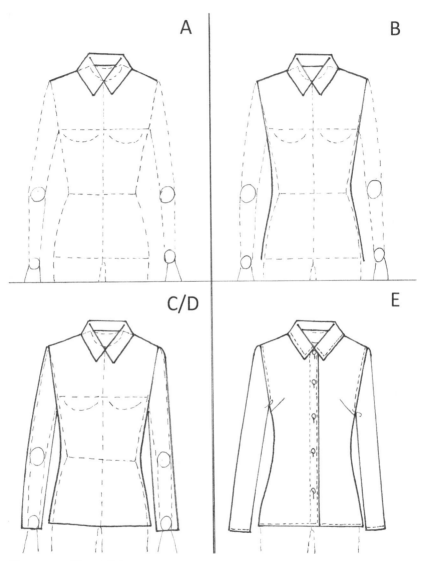

**Figure 3-13:** Fitted Shirt

## Bow Blouse

Here are the steps to drawing a basic bow blouse. This is a basic blouse with the advanced detail of a neck-tie bow. *(Figure 3-14)*

1. Draw a short straight line lightly above the neckline of your croquis, the "Halo" (A).

2. Draw short straight lines that connect the "Halo" to the shoulders (B) and draw a circle (slightly squared) in the Center Front (CF) neck (C).
3. Draw a half circle directly below the CF circle (D). Then draw a second half circle above the CF circle, but with slightly hooked edges (E). Add straight line inside neckline (F).

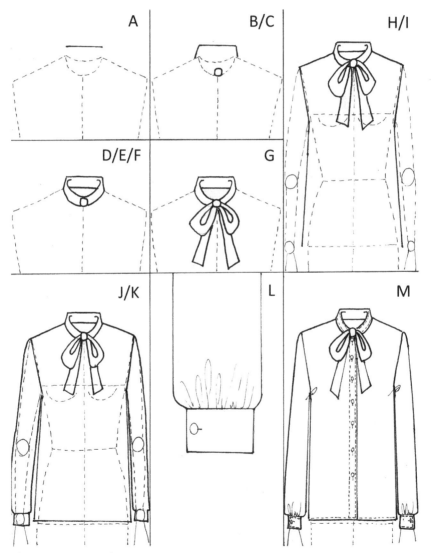

**Figure 3-14:** Bow Blouse

4. Draw the "bow" ties coming from that CF circle (G).

5. Draw the shoulders by just following the shoulder line in your croquis (H). Next, draw the sides of your shirt by drawing a line beginning at the shoulder edge and ending around hip level (I). This line will be straight all the way to the hips.

6. Connect the sides of the shirt with a straight line at the hip area to create the hem (J). Draw the sleeves with straight lines, once again making sure to be slightly away from the croquis' arms (K).

7. Curve your sleeve lines onto a square and add button and shirring detail as necessary (L).

8. Finish off with buttons and stitching details (M).

# How to Draw Knit Tops

Knit tops are the most casual form of shirts and are considered one of the most important aspects of a sportswear clothing line. T-shirts, tank tops, camisoles, hoodies . . . these are all examples of knit tops. If you are thinking of getting a job within this market, it is very important that as an assistant, intern or any other entry-level position, you learn the basics of drawing these items in flat or quick sketch form.

## Drawing a T-Shirt

See Figure 3-15.

1. Draw the shoulder lines (following the shoulders on your croquis) (A).

2. Draw the side seams of your t-shirt by following the side seams of your croquis. If your t-shirt is a snug fitting one, then follow the lines just like your croquis (B).

3. If your t-shirt is a little looser, then draw these lines slightly away from the body of your croquis (C).

4. Draw the neckline of your t-shirt by also tracing the neckline of your croquis (D).

5. If your t-shirt has a neck band, then draw a second curved line under the neckline and also inside the back neckline (E).

6. To create the hem of your t-shirt, draw a straight line that connects your side seam lines (F).

7. Finally, draw the sleeves (G) and add stitch details.

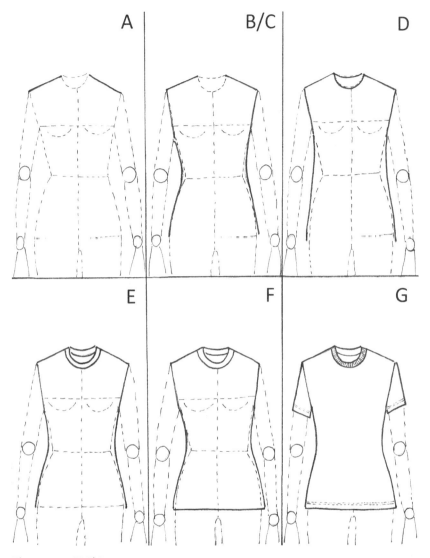

A

B/C

D

E

F

G

**Figure 3-15:** T-Shirt

# It's All in the Details: Drawing Details of Tops

Learning how to sketch details of garments is an essential component of drawing and will really elevate your sketches. The following are my "Nick Tips" on drawing four important details related to tops, shirts, and jackets: Darts and Princess Seams, Buttons, Stitching and Binding. Let's begin with Darts and Princess Seams.

## Darts, Princess Seams

Darts and Princess Seams are construction details, especially specific to woven (non-stretch) garments. While lots of knit clothing may also have darts and princess seams, they are more often found in non-stretchy garments like dress shirts, jackets and coats. *(Figure 3-16)*

Darts are folds that help shape a curved area such as around the bust or to give a more fitted shape to the torso.

Princess seams are also for shape and are seams that divide the front and side of a garment. If you take half of a top and divide it in half again, that halfway mark is considered the princess seam.

### Buttons

Drawing buttons is easy. I call it the "mini lollipop": It is as simple as drawing circles with connecting little lines (A). *(Figure 3-17)*

The important thing you need to know is how and when to draw the button holes. Here's a quick guide: If it is a dress shirt, draw the button holes vertically (up and down) (B).

If it is a jacket or coat, the button holes are usually drawn horizontally. Often, for jackets, you will want to draw the equivalent of a bound button hole. This looks more like a sideways paddle. (C)

### Topstitching

It's very important that when sketching tops, especially knits, you correctly draw the stitching. Topstitching is one of the most important details to add to a technical sketch. It not only elevates your sketch but also adds important information since top stitching is for decoration as well as construction purposes. The iconic Levi's jeans are famously top stitched in a goldenrod color to show pocket elements and give slight design detail (A). *(Figure 3-18)*

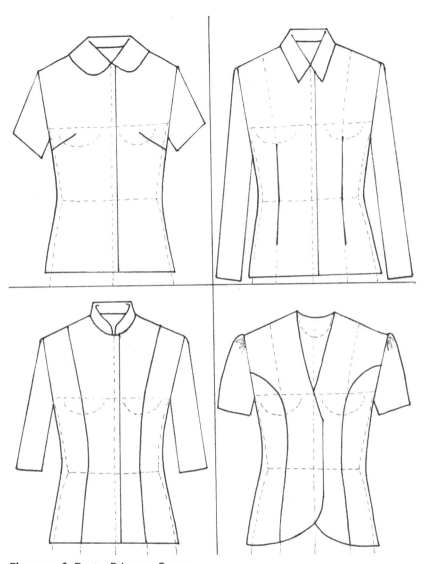

**Figure 3-16:** Darts, Princess Seams

Shirts are top stitched at the hem (B), sleeves (C), collars (D) for reinforcement and as a traditional tailoring technique. This traditional form of topstitching is drawn like little broken lines.

For knit garments (t-shirts, hoodies, tank tops), the stitching normally involves something called a coverstitch. This is drawn as two rows of

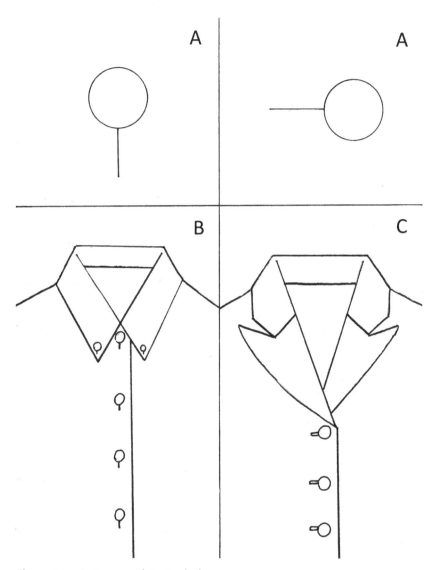

**Figure 3-17:** Buttons and Buttonholes

broken lines (E). Make sure you do the correct stitching for the different type of garment. When in doubt, use this rule:

1.  Woven = Single broken lines.
2.  Knit/Stretchy = Double broken lines.

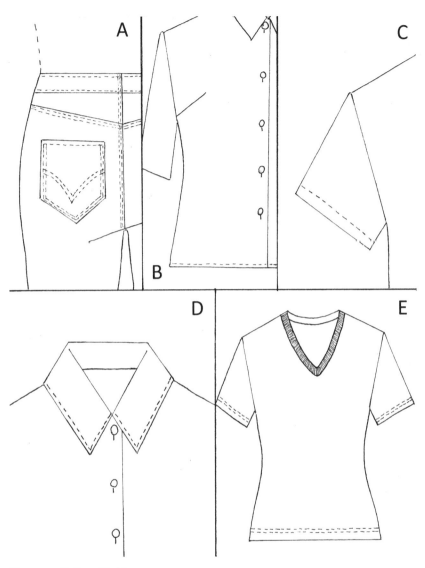

**Figure 3-18:** Topstitching

## Binding

In terms of fashion construction, Binding involves narrow strips of fabric that are folded and sewn usually to edges of a garment, principally (but not exclusively) to knit ones. It is a way to bind and finish these articles of clothing. The way you sketch binding on a knit top is quite simple. Draw a line parallel and very closely to the lines you already sketched as the edges of your garment. That is all you have to do! (A). *(Figure 3-19)*

Now, if you really want to impress your fashion school instructor (or boss at your new design job), do the following: After you have drawn these lines, very carefully, sketch additional broken lines inside these lines. These represent the stitching that occurs when sewing binding to the edges of a knit garment (B).

## Drawing Jackets

Jackets are tailored outer garments worn usually over tops, shirts or blouses. They have sleeves and fasten in the front area, either single breasted or double breasted. Jackets come in a variety of styles and could be woven (non-stretch) or knit (stretch). As I described in the "Drawing Shirts" section of this chapter, many beginners make the mistake of either drawing jackets way too close to the body (following the outer lines of the croquis exactly) or making the jackets too cropped.

Figure 3-20 shows you the right and wrong way to draw a jacket.

## Single Breasted Jacket

1. Start with sketching the notched lapel from Figure 3-10. Connect each lapel with two vertical lines extending slightly below hip (A). *(Figure 3-21)*
2. Next, draw the shoulders by following the shoulder line in your croquis. Because it is a jacket, this time slope up slightly as you get to the outside shoulder area (B). This is to show padding that might be on the shoulders of that jacket. But be careful not to make it look like a quarterback of a football team as you saw on the "DON'T" sketch.
3. Draw straight lines that extend from the shoulder line to the waist area and then slightly curve them around the hips of your croquis and onto the bottom of the jacket (C). Be careful not to

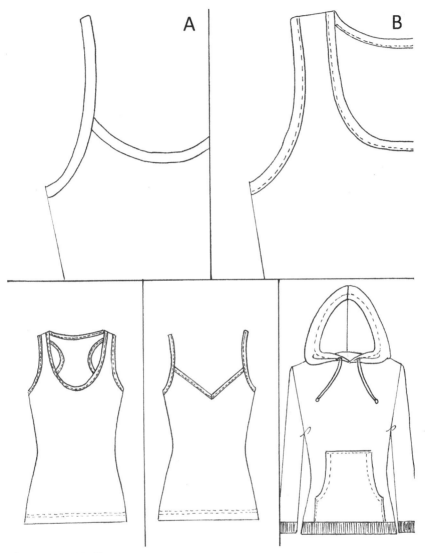

**Figure 3-19:** Binding

follow the same lines of the torso of your croquis; remember that most jackets have a little ease to them and even though they might be deemed "fitted," there is still a little room.

4. Draw the jacket sleeves. Make sure to not follow the lines of your croquis' arms exactly. Remember that a jacket sleeve is

DO          DON'T

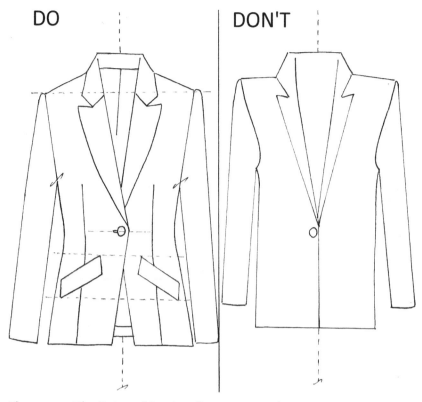

**Figure 3-20:** The Do's and Don'ts of Drawing a Jacket

usually slightly roomier than a knit sleeve. Also, make sure you draw a slight curve at the shoulder cap area (D).

5.  Erase one of the vertical lapel lines to show the crossover of the jacket (E).

6.  Finish the body of your jacket sketch by drawing a straight line to show the hem. (F).

7.  Now it is time to add Darts and/or Princess Seams to your sketch. Tailored garments usually always have darts and/or Princess Seams. Always remember to add these darting details as they are crucial to the construction of the garment (G).

8.  Finally, finish your jacket by drawing the buttons, button holes and pockets. Don't forget my "lollipop" analogy and remember that jacket button holes are drawn as little horizontal lines (H).

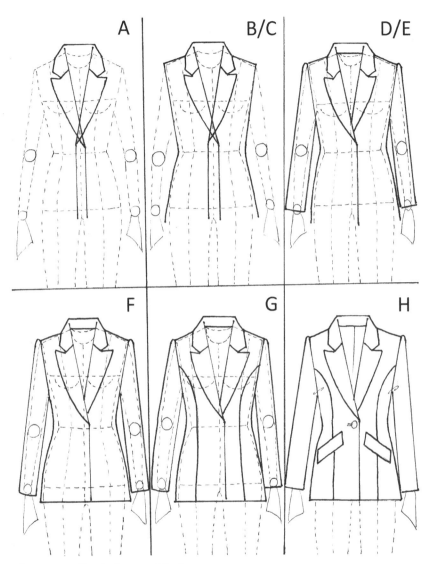

**Figure 3-21:** Single Breasted Jacket

# Drawing Skirts

There are many different types of skirts, all differentiated by silhouette. They include Straight, A-line, Circle, Full and Tulip styles. In my lesson here, I will give you a few quick tips on how to draw three of those skirts, the Straight/Pencil, A-Line/Flared and Full Skirt.

# Straight or Pencil Skirt

The Straight Skirt—sometimes called the "Pencil" skirt—is just what the name says it is: A straight, lean skirt. It's a simple garment to draw since there is not much to it. *(Figure 3-22)*

1. Using your croquis under your sketching paper, you will concentrate on the bottom half, beginning at the waist. As with drawing any skirt (or pant, as well), figure out if your garment begins at the "Natural Waist" (the belly button area) or below it (low-slung).
2. Following my "Waist Rule": If your garment begins at the natural waist, then draw a straight horizontal line at that level (using your croquis as a guide) which will represent the waist (A).
3. If it is a low slung skirt draw a slightly curved line about ⅛" to ¼" below the natural waist (B). Now, if your skirt is very low-slung, you could draw that line lower, of course, but not too low!
4. Next, draw the sides of the skirt by sketching curved lines down the side of the legs on your croquis (C). These lines will end depending on what length you want your skirt to be. I'm doing a knee length skirt, so obviously, my drawing will end at the knee.
5. Connect these lines at the bottom to draw the hem of the skirt (D).
6. Finally, add darts at the waist by drawing short vertical lines about ½" in length at the Princess line of your croquis and a side zipper denoted by broken stitches and a small loop (E).

# A-Line or Flared Skirt

An A-line skirt is one that is usually fitted at the waist, then skims the hips and flares out from there to create the outlines of the letter "A," therefore the name "A-line." *(Figure 3-23)*

1. Draw the waist using the same instructions from the Straight Skirt (A).
2. Draw the sides of your flared skirt by sketching lines that jut out from the waist, skimming the hips of your croquis and continue down diagonally creating an "A" shape (B). End these lines at the length you desire your skirt to be.

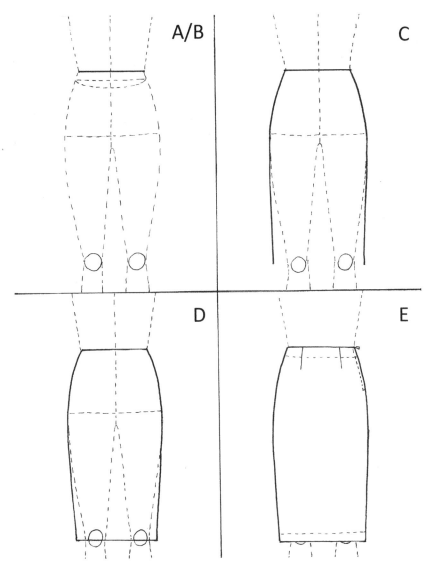

**Figure 3-22:** Straight or Pencil Skirt

3. Connect these lines with a slightly curved line to form the hem of the skirt (C).
4. If you want to add details, you can draw a second line parallel to the waistline, right below it, to give it a waistband, as well as pockets and zipper (D).

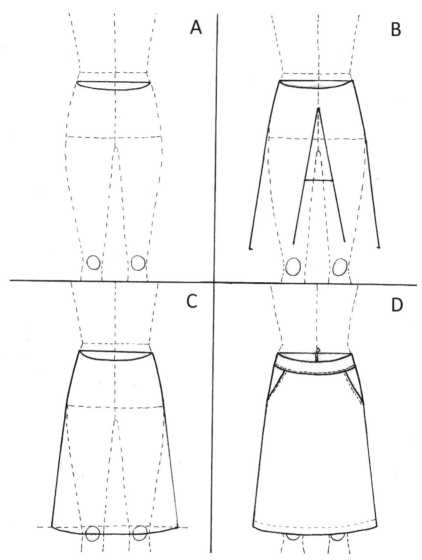

**Figure 3-23:** A-Line or Flared Skirt

# Full Skirt

A Full Skirt is usually created by using a large rectangle of fabric and gathering that material at the waist. It is similar to the A-line, but more voluminous. Here are my "Nick Tips" on how to draw a Full Skirt, with gathers and fullness at the hem. (*Figure 3-24*)

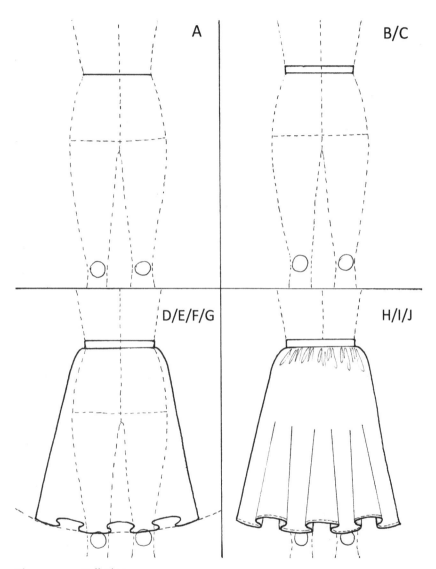

**Figure 3-24:** Full Skirt

1. Draw a straight line at the waist area (A).
2. Draw another line parallel to this line about ¼" above it (B).
3. Connect these lines with short vertical lines (C). You have just drawn a waistband, which the full skirt will be attached to.

4.  Next, it is time to draw the sides of your Full Skirt. Draw two lines that come out of the waistband. They will be slightly curved in shape and continue down diagonally (D). A good rule of thumb is to extend these lines about 1" away from your croquis' legs (E).
5.  Now, it is time to draw the hem. First draw a curved line as seen in (F). This line will be erased later, therefore my suggestion is to do it lightly.
6.  Right on top of that line, draw curves as seen in (G).
7.  Then, draw lines as seen in (H).
8.  You can erase that first lightly drawn line that you did when you drew the curved hem line (I).
9.  Finally, draw the gathers (J).

# It's All in the Details: Drawing Details of a Skirt

## Ruffles

Ruffles come in handy, especially if you are drawing a fuller skirt, gown, or sleeve. Always pay special attention to the type of fabric you want to portray. For example, ruffles in taffeta will be bigger and bolder than the small, delicate ruffles in a chiffon dress. With that being said, my "Nick Tip" on how to always draw a perfect ruffle and/or flounce can be applied to all drawings with just a few alterations. *(Figure 3-25)*

1.  Let's say that you have already drawn your skirt, and want to add a ruffle at the bottom (A).
2.  Draw two short lines extending out from the sides of the hem of your skirt. These lines can be short or long, depending on the width of your ruffles, but will always be shaped like slanted upside down "J's" (B).
3.  Connect these lines with a lightly drawn curved line. (Draw this line lightly since it will be erased later.) (C)
4.  Now, it is time to draw the "ruffle" flounces or curves. To do this, draw small s-shaped curves like in (D).
5.  Then draw lines that touch the inner and outer lines of these small s-shaped lines (E).
6.  Finally, erase that original curved hem line that you sketched lightly (F).

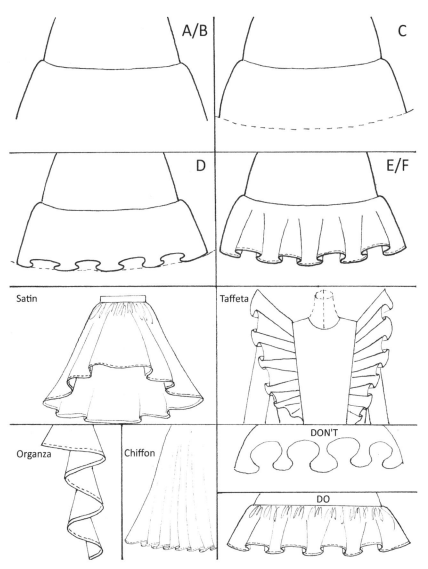

**Figure 3-25:** Ruffles

## Gathering

Gathering is a sewing technique that takes a certain amount of fabric and gathers it, thereby shortening the original length and creating small puckers. This gathered piece is usually then attached to a non-gathered section. The word "shirring" is also used interchangeably with the word "gathering"; they mean the same thing. Drawing gathering seems easy enough—compared to other fashion details or garments, but you would not believe how many of my beginning sketching students would constantly get it wrong. The following will be my "Nick Tip" to drawing Gathers. Practice this over and over again and soon enough, you will perfect your gathering-drawing skills. *(Figure 3-26)*

1. Draw a straight line (A).
2. Touching that straight line, lightly draw loops and mini m-shapes with a slight flare to them, think of curved "sassy" m's (B). Make sure the tops of those so-called mini-m's touch the straight line, but ever so lightly.
3. Do this over and over again. Practice will make perfect. Trust me.
4. Now, add your newly-learned technique to a skirt waist (C), or ruffled hem (D).

# Drawing Pants

Like many other garments, there are various types of pants including Fitted, Skinny, Wide-leg/Palazzo, Boot-cut, Bell-bottom, Culottes, Shorts, Knickers, and so on. Even though these are all varied styles, there are common denominators that can be used when drawing all types of pants. Once you have mastered the basics, you can then move on to designing any silhouette your creative mind can imagine. Below are my "Nick Tips" on sketching the most popular styles.

## Fitted Pants

1. As you did when drawing the waist of your skirts, decide if your pants will begin at the natural waist or be low-slung (below the waist). If your pants begin at the natural waist, draw a straight line (A). If your pants are low-slung, then draw a slightly curved line about ¼" below the natural waist (B). *(Figure 3-27)*
2. Draw a vertical line down the center of your croquis, from the waist line and ending at the crotch point. What you should have

**Figure 3-26:** Gathering

now is something that resembles a T (C). Draw a short, slightly
diagonal line at the crotch; this short line signifies the front (D).

3. Now it is time to draw the pant legs. Start with the outseam or
   outside edge of the pants. Begin drawing a line from the waist

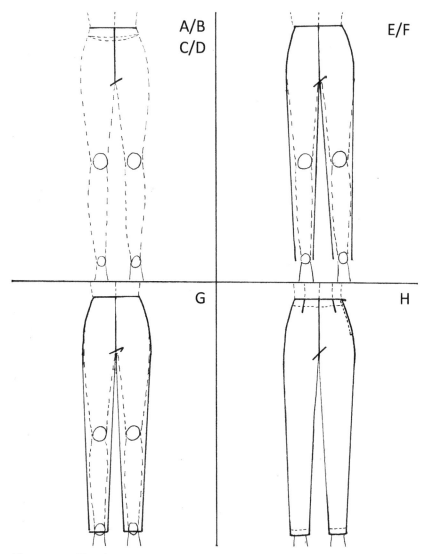

**Figure 3-27:** Fitted Pants

and following the curve of the hips. After you've made your curved hip, take your ruler and draw a straight line slightly away from the outer edges of your croquis' legs, down to the ankle (E).

4. Now, draw the inseam (inner edge) of the pants. Do this by drawing a straight line from the crotch down to the hem slightly away from the inner part of your croquis' legs (F).

5. Connect these two lines with a short straight line, thereby creating the hem of your pants (G).

6. Add darts to the waist by drawing short lines approximately ½" long following the Princess lines in your croquis and stitching details if applicable (H).

## Leggings and Skinny Pants

Leggings and Skinny Pants might seem like a very simple silhouette to draw, but there are common mistakes that make these garments look incorrect. A few simple corrections can elevate your sketch from amateur to amazing! *(Figure 3-28)*

1. The first mistake that is commonly made when drawing leggings, is to create a "V" at the crotch. While this does denote that the pants are tight, it also shows that the pants are TOO tight. It's not only improper sketching but it also demonstrates improper fit.

2. Similar to the front, the same mistake is often made for the back of the pants. Instead of making two rounded half circles (which overemphasize the rear end), make a slanted line. This will be longer than the line used for the front rise and will delineate the front from the back and show proper fit.

3. The final mistake often made when sketching leggings is to draw an exact outline of the croquis leg. While they might often look that tight on a body, they do not look the same on a hanger at the store. When illustrating flat sketches, it is most important to mimic the garment off the body or "flat," to best demonstrate the technical details. *(Figure 3-29)*

So, now that you know how NOT to draw Leggings/Skinny Pants, here are my "Nick Tips" on how to draw them properly: *(Figure 3-30)*

1. Draw the waist. Remember my "Waist Rule": Straight line if the pants begin at the natural waist (A). If the waist is low-slung, draw a slightly curved line about ¼" below your croquis' waist (B).

2. Draw a vertical line down the center front to create the rise (C).

3. Draw a short slightly diagonal line at the crotch point to signify the front (D).

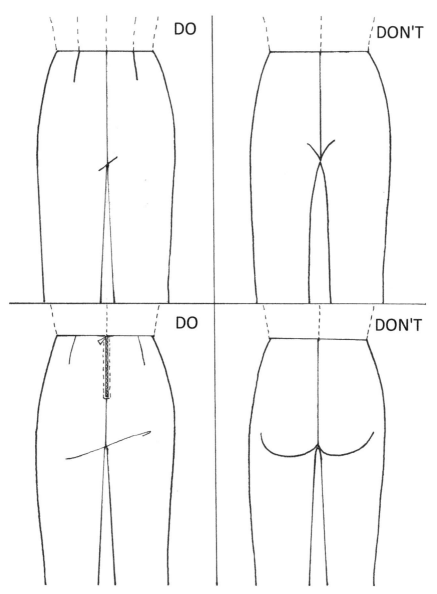

**Figure 3-28:** The Do's and Don'ts of Drawing the Front and Back of a Pant Rise

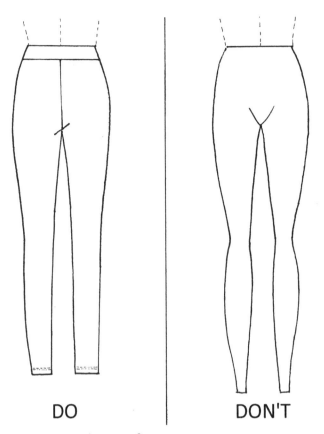

DO                    DON'T

**Figure 3-29:** The Do and Don't of Drawing Leggings

4. For the outseam, take your ruler and draw a line right on the outside edge of the leg of your croquis, almost tracing the leg but not too close! (E) For the inseam, do the same—draw a line, starting from the crotch and ending at the ankle. This line will skim the inner leg of your croquis and basically be straight. (F).

5. Next, connect these two lines with short horizontal lines to form the hem (G).

6. Finish your pants with details such as a waistband and topstitching (H).

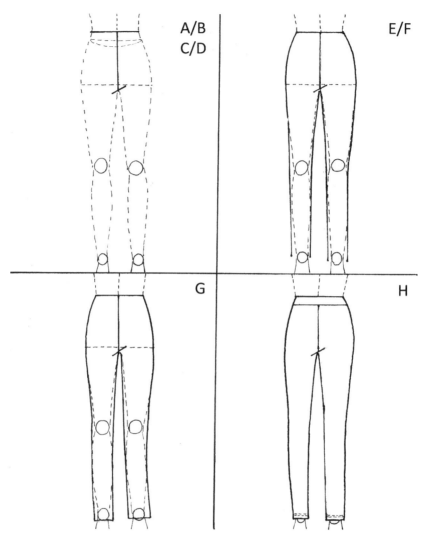

**Figure 3-30:** Leggings and Skinny Pants

## Flared Pants

Flared pants are drawn like a fitted pant from the waist down to the knees but then from there, a flare is added. The flare can be gradual, thereby sketching a "boot cut" silhouette or more severe which then becomes the infamous bell bottoms. Here are the steps for the basic flared pants: *(Figure 3-31)*

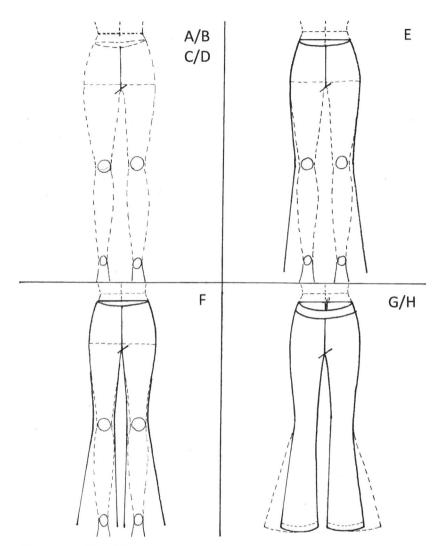

A/B
C/D

E

F

G/H

**Figure 3-31:** Flared Pants

1. Draw the waist. Remember my "Waist Rule": Straight line if the pants begin at the natural waist (A). If the waist is low-slung, draw a slightly curved line about ¼" below your croquis' waist (B).
2. Draw a straight vertical line down the center front to create the rise (C).

3. Draw a short slightly diagonal line at the crotch point to signify the front (D).

4. Now it is time to draw the pant legs. For the outseam, take your pencil (and a ruler to guide you) and follow the line of the outside edge of the leg, essentially almost tracing it from underneath. Once you get near the knee, begin flaring it outwards, in a straight line, and end at the ankle or below the ankle of your croquis (E).

5. For the inseam, draw a line starting from the crotch and ending at the ankle (F). This line will skim the inner leg of your croquis and basically be straight with a very slight flare at the bottom.

6. Connect the outseam and inseam with a slightly curved line (G). Finish your flared pants with any waistband detail appropriate to the style of pant you are creating (H).

## Wide-Leg/Palazzo Pants

1. Begin drawing your Wide-leg pants the same way you begin all your other pants: By sketching the waist line. Remember to follow my "Waist Sketching Rule": For the natural waist, draw a straight line (A). If your pants are low-slung, then draw a slightly curved line about ¼" below the natural waist (B). *(Figure 3-32)*

2. Draw a straight vertical line down the center front to create the rise. You should now have something that resembles a T (C).

3. Add a short slightly diagonal line at the crotch point to signify the front (D).

4. Now it is time to create the Palazzo Pant legs. Let's start with the outseam or outside edge of the pants. From the waist, take your ruler and draw a straight line diagonally and away from your croquis until you reach the ankle. This line should end about ¾" to 1" away from the foot of your croquis (E).

5. Next, draw the inseam (inner edge) of the pants. Do this by drawing a straight line from the crotch to the ankle. There is no flare or curve to this line. All the fullness was already created by the outseam (F).

6. Connect these two lines with a slightly curved line, thereby creating the hem of your pants (G).

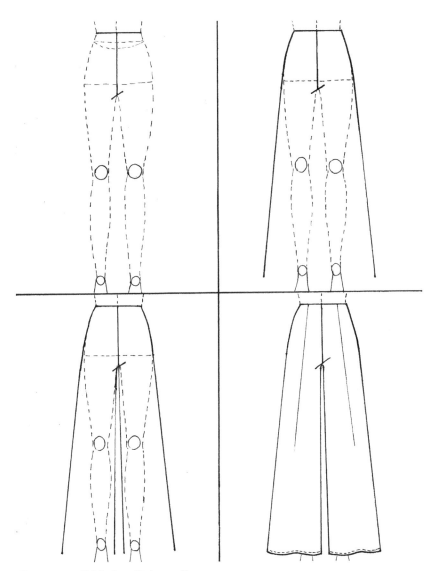

**Figure 3-32:** Wide-Leg/Palazzo Pants

7. After you have drawn both pant legs, you will notice that there is a small space between the two legs. A common mistake is to have the pant legs connect. This is incorrect and technically inaccurate. As I stated above, the sweep of the pant leg is created entirely by the outseam (H).

# Drawing Dresses

Dresses come in a variety of silhouettes and styles. In the fashion industry, we use many terms to describe the bountiful variety of dress silhouettes: Shift Dress, Sheath Dress, Column, Ballgown, A-line and Fit-and-Flare, to name just a few. A good way to understand the process of designing a dress is to think of it in two parts: A bodice and a skirt. When you combine these two elements you have a dress. So, now that you have learned the basics of drawing a top and skirt, dresses will be a cinch! *(Figure 3-33)*

## Fitted Sheath Dress

To illustrate how to draw the basics of almost any dress, I will demonstrate by showing you the essential elements of a fitted sheath dress:

1. Begin drawing your dress by sketching the neckline. For this dress, I will sketch a "boat" neckline, which is near the neck (A). *(Figure 3-34)*
2. Now draw the shoulder seams by tracing directly on the shoulders of your croquis but stopping just short of the edge (B).
3. Next draw the armholes by connecting you shoulder seam to the underarm of your croquis. Notice that this line is slightly inside the line of your croquis and curves gently to the underarm (C).
4. Now draw the side seams of your dress by tracing the body of your croquis. Make sure you line is slightly away from the body, especially at the waist (E). Then, take your ruler and draw a straight line ending approximately at the knee (F).
5. Connect the sides of your dress with a straight line, signifying the hem (G).
6. Draw darts and stitching details as needed (H).

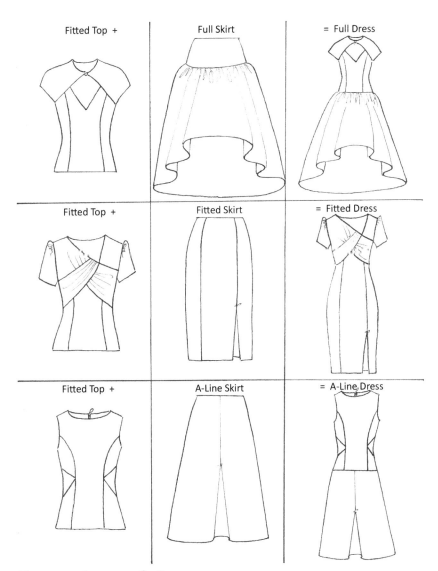

**Figure 3-33:** Anatomy of a Dress

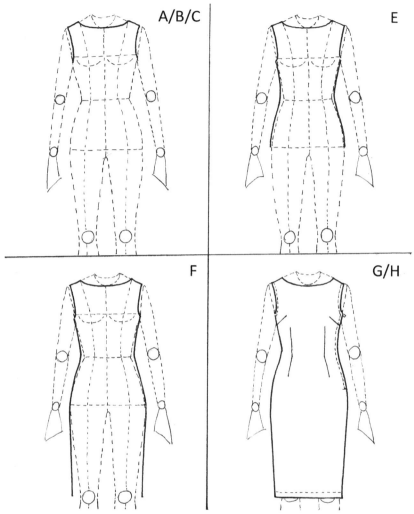

**Figure 3-34:** Fitted Sheath Dress

# Mirror, Mirror... the Folding Method of Drawing

For many beginning fashion sketch artists, it is sometimes difficult to get what we call a "mirror image." I have found, while teaching my students in technical sketching classes, that many of them had trouble with making the right side of a garment look the same as the left; or vice versa. If you are one of those people, I have a "Nick Trick" for you: Fold It! *(Figure 3-35)*

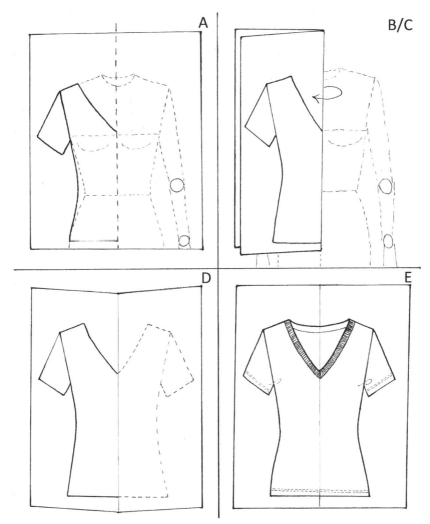

**Figure 3-35:** The Folding Method of Drawing

Let's say that you are trying to draw a basic top:

1. Using your croquis, draw one side of your garment (A).
2. Take your croquis away from underneath and fold your sketching paper in half, directly at the center of your drawing (B).
3. Now trace the other side of the garment (on the wrong side of your paper) using the lines you have already drawn for the first side (C).

4. Open your paper and on the right side of the paper, trace out the lines (D). That's it! You are done! You now have a perfectly symmetrical technical sketch (E).

While you would not want to use this trick for finished assignments or portfolio sketches, it is a great learning tool and something you can do over and over to help improve your skills. Practice makes perfect and soon enough you will be able to draw your sketches without having to use the folding trick.

## Drawing Faces

Drawing a beautiful and detailed face is key in elevating your fashion illustration to the next level. One of the most important points to remember is that symmetry is crucial. If the balance is off only slightly, you will go from cute to crazy in a hot minute! Follow my "Nick Tips" below, and you will be sure to draw the perfect face every time. *(Figure 3-36)*

1. Before you begin sketching a face, do the following: Draw an oval on a piece of heavy card stock paper. This oval should be about 3¾" long and 2⅛" wide. Cut out this oval as a template.
2. Trace the oval template on a regular piece of paper. This will be your "face" (A).
3. Draw a vertical line down the middle of the oval (B). Then draw a horizontal line across the oval, dividing it half. Label this line "½" (C).
4. Now divide again into ¼ sections, both vertically and horizontally (D).
5. At the halfway line, draw the eyes (E) and ears (F).
6. Approximately ⅛ above the eyes, draw the eyebrows (G).
7. Directly above the lower ¼ line, draw the nostrils of the nose (H).
8. Now you are ready to draw the lips right above the halfway point between your chin and nostrils (I).
9. Right above the top 1/4 section, begin drawing the hairline (J).
10. You can now fill in all the details, by completing the hair, nose lines, and slightly squaring the oval as seen in (K). You now have a perfectly symmetrical face!

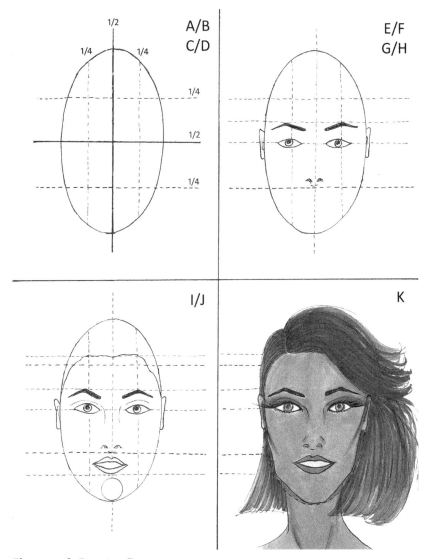

**Figure 3-36:** Drawing Faces

# Shading

Another essential component in drawing a proper fashion illustration, is being able to properly shade your sketch. Shading can be complicated, especially to beginners of fashion sketching. But there is a method to this technique. In my many years of sketching, I admit that I had

**Figure 3-37:** Shading

maddening frustration at getting my shading just right and especially in the right places. So, for those beginning fashion sketchers, I have a "Nick Trick" for basic shading that should work for most of your fashion illustrations. *(Figure 3-37)*

1. When you draw a fashion croquis, or fashion illustration, these drawings are less "flat" and with more dimension. Think of a fashion sketch like a rectangular tube.

2. Here is a basic shading rule: If the light source (the direction of the light) starts from the LEFT, then most of your shading will be done on the RIGHT, or vice versa (A).

3. Now, apply this to a Fashion Illustration with clothing. Notice that when the light is coming from the RIGHT, you will not only be shading the LEFT side of the illustration, but you will also need to pay attention to the folds, shirring and seams of the garment (B).

Hopefully, you have learned a few "Nick Tips" on the fundamentals of sketching for basic flat and fashion illustrations. I have tried to make it as easy as possible and I definitely think that if you are armed with my sketching tricks you will be able to improve your skills tremendously. Whether you are preparing to enroll in fashion school or just looking to improve your drawing technique, I can guarantee that people will definitely be asking: "Where did you learn to draw fashion flats so well?" Just tell them Nick taught you!

# CHAPTER 4

# Getting The Most Out of Fashion School

Now that you are prepared and are ready to start your journey, it is time to give you a few of my "Nick Tips" on how to get the most out of actually attending fashion school. Throughout my time as a Fashion Instructor, Lecturer and speaking to fashion students across the country, I have compiled a few suggestions that will help you maximize your education. Hopefully these directives will help you get the most out of all the opportunities that a fashion education can offer. As I like to tell my students, "No Should've, Would've, Could've . . . Just Do It!

## Focus Your Energy on What You Don't Know

Everyone has their strengths and weaknesses. As I have stated, I was confident with my drawing skills, while feeling a bit inadequate in sewing and construction. My immediate instinct when entering fashion school was to take all the drawing and sketching classes that they had to offer. I wanted to perfect my skill and show off my talent. I soon realized what a mistake that was. When I received my classes for the first semester, I discovered that there was a lot for me to learn. I had a curriculum filled with patternmaking, draping, fashion textiles, and costing. I was finding out that if I didn't focus on educating myself in all the other disciplines in the fashion world, I would never become the designer I aspired to be. It is natural to be afraid of what you don't know, but do not disregard what is difficult for you and run away from it. Embrace it and soon you will conquer your fears and reach your goals. That is what will make you a success in the fashion industry.

## Find a Classmate Buddy

Because of my fear and anxiety in not being a sewing genius, I found a fellow student who was one. Her name was Wendy and she had extensive knowledge and experience in sewing and construction. I immediately turned to her for help and extra "You Can Do It!" guidance. Guess what she wasn't so amazing at? Sketching and draping: the two things I loved and that came naturally to me. So in return for her sewing guidance, I reciprocated by always being right by her side during our draping and sketching classes. One could say that we used each other—but for good! She made me better and I (hopefully) did the same for her. So, my "Nick Tip" here is to find a classmate buddy who can help with your fashion school inadequacies and you can help them back, if they need it. Trust me, it will make your time in fashion school just a little less stressful.

## Stand Out

I bet that when you saw the words "Stand Out," you thought I was referring to what you wear and how you dress to class. And yes, you are slightly correct in this. It's never bad to create your own fashion identity with your own personal style and while this will not give you an "A" in your patternmaking class, at least it will make your fellow classmates—and sometimes, instructors—know who you are. This can be a plus or minus. In my years of teaching, I had many students who dressed fabulously and had stupendous personal style, but couldn't finish an assignment on time if their life depended on it. They looked great, but I wondered how they even got into college, besides just appearing to be fashionable and cute. With that being said, if you are able to express your own personal style and be a good student, you are definitely on the right track to being a success. In this day and age, a fashion designer's self-image, fortunately or unfortunately, can be as important as their designs.

But, what I really mean when I say "Stand Out," is your participation in class. I have found that the most successful students and fashion entrepreneurs, always give 110% to every assignment they have. When an instructor or employer gives you an assignment, think to yourself how you can accomplish it successfully, while giving 10% more than what is asked of you. By just adding a little bonus to every task that you are assigned, you will easily be a standout to not only your instructor, but also the entire class. I will inject a personal anecdote involving my time in fashion school that worked for me and that I passed down to all the students in my class. In most, if not all, of my draping, sewing and/or patternmaking classes, when it came time to sew a garment, we the students were provided with muslin. Muslin is unbleached cotton; it is used for draping your designs on a model form and most often, the actual fabric you would use to complete an assignment. For example, after draping a basic bodice, skirt or dress, you would then cut the garment in the bland cotton muslin fabric and sew your assigned item of clothing. After a few of those assignments and seeing nineteen other bland muslin garments created by my fellow students, I had a bright idea: why not use real fabric?

I went to the bargain-basement section of my local fabric store and found $1.99 per yard fabric (after all, I was a starving student!) in bold colors, fun prints and textiles that were much more visually exciting than the plain muslin provided to us. I will never forget arriving to class and presenting my red and white polka dot dress next to all the other basic muslin dresses. It sure got my instructor's attention and made me a standout! I must stress, however, that before you "Go Bold," you might want to ask for your teacher's permission. While I certainly enjoyed my big reveal to the entire class, a conversation with the educator will ensure that your plan to get ahead doesn't backfire! Oh, and needless to say, I remember many of my fellow classmates followed suit and began doing the same thing—ditching the muslin in lieu of real fabric in an effort to stand out more.

Stand Out! Student Projects in Printed and Colored Fabrics

When I taught my draping and patternmaking classes at FIDM, I wholeheartedly told my students to do as I did back in the day, and take their garments to the next level. To my delight, on the day a jacket or dress drape was due, I would walk into a room gloriously filled with garments in a varied range of colored and printed fabrications. It was not only more exciting to look at, but also much more motivating to create.

Going the extra mile and standing out in fashion school can be applied to all your courses and projects. You can take the real fabric vs. muslin example and use it for all your classes. Ask your instructor if you can do "something extra" for a particular trend presentation; when doing an assignment on a noteworthy designer, find out from the fashion school's archives if in fact they might have an actual garment from that designer and have the college museum's curator bring it in to class as part of your presentation. Standing out might also just simply be about attaching actual fabric swatches to your sketching homework or researching new and creative ways to display your trend boards. Whatever the class, or whatever assignment you are tasked to complete, there is always a way to push yourself to give at least 10% more. Be creative and proactive, and you will surely be a standout in everything you do.

# Keep a Humble Folder

A great piece of advice someone gave me a long time ago, was to keep a humble folder. While attending school, you will be assigned to complete what seems like hundreds upon hundreds of projects. Some of those assignments will be successful, while many others will seem destined for the garbage bin. Our instinct is always to keep the good while tossing out the bad, but my philosophy is to fight the urge. Take every unsuccessful sketch and garment that you create, and make a separate folder or box. While you might not be thrilled to see it fill up with work that you find inferior, when you revisit those projects years later, you will be amazed and truly inspired with how much growth you have achieved.

While I was a student, I was honored enough to be accepted into the college's Advanced Fashion Design Program, which enrolls only ten students for an extra intensive year. During that grueling time, our main goal was to create our very first collection that was to be debuted in a spectacular fashion show at the conclusion of the year. That very first collection is really my ultimate "Nick Humble Folder." For months and months, I made every single one of those designs and there were many sleepless nights attached to each of those pieces, not to mention the sweat and tears. They were so badly sewn, I'm surprised they made it onto a runway. More importantly, looking at them reminds me of how far I have come and how much I have grown as a designer. Your humble folder is not meant to embarrass you or make you feel bad about yourself. Quite the contrary; it is there to show you how far you have come and to motivate you to be the best designer you can be.

Humble Nick: FIDM Debut Fashion Illustration

# Do Everything

While you might think that "Standing Out" and "Giving 110%" are the same as "Doing Everything," this bit of advice specifically addresses opportunities that arise in the form of internships and one-off jobs. While you are attending fashion school, you will have many opportunities to enhance your already full workload. These prospects can appear in many forms. They range from working as a dresser, assisting a PR company putting on a fashion show, or even helping a designer at a look book photo shoot. Check in with your college's career center and ask, ask, ask! Find out any time there are opportunities such as the aforementioned and do it all! For the most part, these might not be paid jobs but who cares! They're invaluable to your fashion school experience. A seemingly inconsequential one-day job as a steamer or dresser for a fashion event is a way for you to learn how to properly handle clothes. Working backstage allows you to see all the behind-the-scenes action and learn what it takes to mount a fashion show—something that you might need to do for your own clothing line one day. Everything leads to something and little jobs like these—especially in the fashion industry—are like nutrients to your fashion soul and will make you a better student and eventually, a better fashion designer.

I remember when I was a student, I would check the "job board" every week to see if dressers, steamers or assistants were needed for fashion shows. I annoyed the heck out of the career center because I was always there, like an eager-beaver. Out of these opportunities, two incredible memories come to mind. The first one involved 90s supermodels! I was alerted by my trusty career center about a call for help at a fashion show occurring at the iconic Grauman's Chinese Theater in Hollywood. It turned out to be a huge VIP Isaac Mizrahi Fashion Show fundraiser. Along with my fellow FIDM classmate who came with me, we steamed in a lonely room for hours. We were literally the only two people in a gigantic room filled with racks of clothing. I have to be honest, my friend and I were on the verge of saying "What is the point? And what are we learning here?" We were about to leave (nobody would have noticed) when an assistant came rushing into the room and shouted "Follow me! We need more dressers!" We were quickly ushered backstage and assigned a rack of clothes to continue steaming. Soon after, the models began to fill the room, including Linda Evangelista, Naomi Campbell, Christy Turlington (it was 1992 after all!) and all the top supermodels that were plastered across my apartment walls! And if that wasn't enough, I was assigned to dress the one-and-only Kate Moss. I literally had a Fashion Heart Attack and was in Fashion Heaven . . . at the same time. It became one of my Top Ten Most Memorable Moments of my time at fashion school.

The second anecdote involved a non-paid dresser job that, once again, my FIDM career counselor alerted me to. Since it was another non-paid, lowly dresser job, no one really wanted to do it. But I raised my hand and said "I will!" It turned out to be a Karl Lagerfeld trunk show at the Neiman Marcus in Beverly Hills. A half hour into my steaming duties, lo and behold, THE Karl Lagerfeld appeared (it was a surprise to everyone, except maybe the directors of the Neiman Marcus PR department) and proceeded to give us an impromptu mentoring session for the next fifteen minutes. And guess what one of his suggestions was? Yep: Do Everything. Amen, Kaiser Karl.

# Instagram/Blog

My next piece of advice is more of a modern one and involves a little bit of social media, and in particular Instagram and blogs. I am certain that most students attending a fashion school probably already have an Instagram profile, filled with selfies. Well, here's a novel idea: every now and then, take a temporary break from you and focus on your school designs. In other words, take photos of some of your assignments that include sketching, sewing, draping and/or patternmaking class and post them on Instagram.

As a fashion school student, I think it's great for your friends, family and people out in the Instagram-sphere to get to see your designs and what you are doing. In fact, I follow several fashion school students who post great photos of their illustrations as well as garments they completed for a project. I love seeing what aspiring fashion designers are working on. It's motivational to me and for the student, it is like keeping a diary of your time in school. And as a bonus, your parents can see that you are really working on in fashion school—as opposed to, well, not.

The blog suggestion is another way for a fashion student to keep a diary of your time. It can also serve as an online portfolio and can be beneficial in the future in terms of getting a job. And definitely, if you are studying visual communications or styling at a fashion school, having your own blog should be *de rigeur*. Having a "Fashion Blog" is like an addendum to your portfolio.

# Portfolio: From Drab to Fab

One of the final and most essential tools that you will gain from attending fashion school is the all-important portfolio. The portfolio will be your gateway into the fashion world and critical in getting you employment. A good portfolio is a make it or break it element to a successful career in fashion.

So what is a portfolio and more importantly, what makes a good one? Think of your portfolio as a Visual Resume. It should tell a story about what you can do, what your design ideas are, and most importantly your originality. A good frame of reference would be to compare a designer's portfolio to that of a model. When interviewing models for a fashion show or photo shoot, models come in and they bring a portfolio with photos of themselves, showing different looks, different situations and genres. It gives the casting director or fashion designer, who is conducting the interview, a peek into what the model can achieve. It's the same concept for an aspiring Fashion Designer. A young fashion designer's portfolio needs to be visually stimulating, creative and most importantly, show off your talent to your future employer.

Modern fashion portfolios are now composed of two parts: a web portfolio and a traditional physical version. While attending fashion school, you will undoubtedly have to take a Portfolio Class, so you'll get suggestions from your instructor on how to have the best portfolio for the right job. But in addition to this, I wanted to give you some of my tried-and-true suggestions to make your portfolio the best it can be so you are well-prepared when it is time to go job hunting.

# Nick Tips

A good portfolio needs to be professional, concise, clean and reflect your ideas and talent. Here are my "Nick Tips" on creating the perfect portfolio.

## Buy a Proper Portfolio

Walking into a job interview with a manila folder filled with drawings is definitely the wrong way to go and will reflect poorly on who you are and how seriously you take the job prospect. Visit your local art store and check out the portfolio section. Portfolios come in many different sizes.

I actually began with a rather large portfolio simply because most of my fashion school work was done on rather large paper, 14" × 17". This worked fine for the first couple of interviews, until I realized I may need to downsize. Time and time again, I would walk into an interview and my prospective employer's desk would be filled with their own work or just too small to accommodate my grand assortment. You could see the strain on their faces as they placed this oversized and cumbersome portfolio on top of their already crowded table. I quickly realized that it was not about the size of the portfolio that mattered, (I thought Bigger was Better!) but the quality and creativity of the work inside. I soon decided to purchase a second portfolio that would hold 8 ½" × 11" sketches and photos and would therefore be easier to present and also carry from interview to interview. With the presentation of that physical portfolio, you can also bring with you a DVD copy of your work or you might impress your future boss with a business card that has a web address to your website or blog that they can visit in the future in order to make their final decision on job placement.

## The Essentials in Your Portfolio: Cover Page

Begin with a clean cover page, with your name and all essential information. You could keep this simple or begin with a fabulous fashion illustration to make a great first impression.

## Keep a Keen and Objective Eye

One of the hardest things about putting together a portfolio is the editing process. The excitement of accomplishing so much during your time in fashion school can often lead to a slightly subjective view of your own work. Often, it is hard to tell which are your accomplishments and which are . . . well, the stinkers! Get advice from your most trusted or favorite instructor. When I was trying to decide what to put in my first portfolio, I asked my fashion illustration instructor for her input on what she liked best in terms of my work. Besides being an incredibly gifted and world renowned sketch artist herself, I knew that she understood what was needed to go in a portfolio and that she would be honest and direct.

## Start with a Mood/Inspiration Page

A mood or inspiration page is one of the essential components in your Fashion Design portfolio. Besides being an impacting visual, it is always nice to show an employer your inspiration for the sketches or collection that you are presenting in your portfolio. This inspiration page should be in collage form. In addition, one of my most important "Nick Tips" is to never put other designer's fashion or runway photos in your collage. Why not? Because you may risk the chance that those photos from that designer might actually be far more interesting and better than your own designs. Instead, use photos from a décor magazine, paintings, architecture, nature, jewelry, and iconic style muses from history. A mood page should show the viewer a glimpse into your creativity and unique ideas without showing actual fashion. Leave the sketches and fashion editorials for a different part of your portfolio.

## Group Sketches

A portfolio will change as you gain more experience in the industry, but when first entering the workforce after graduating from fashion school, the best way to show your potential to your future employer is through sketches. These sketches will make up the bulk of your portfolio. What I find works best and makes for a cohesive presentation is to categorize your sketches into groups. These mini-collections should correspond with your mood/inspiration page and should also include flat sketches. Often, you will have these groupings from school assignments or will be

**Figure 4-1:** Fashion Group Sketch

able to create a mini-collection from projects you already have. In addition, you should include several of these mini-collections in a portfolio
to show a variety; a range of what you can design. *(Figure 4-1)*

## Flat Sketches

Also included in your portfolio should be flat sketches that correspond to the fashion sketches of that mini-collection. The reason for adding a flat sketch (also referred to as a technical sketch) is twofold: It shows that you have a grasp of garment construction and that you know how to do technical sketches. Often, this is the most important aspect in your

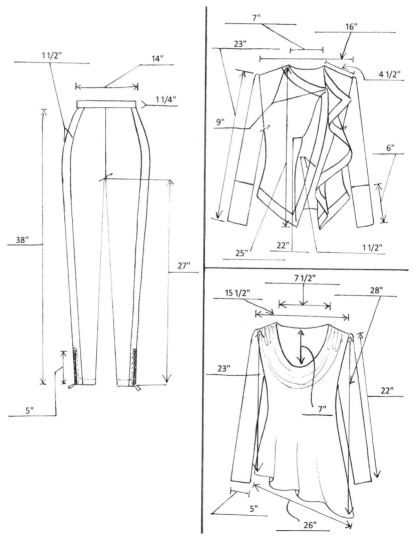

**Figure 4-2:** Flat Sketch with Detailed Measurements

portfolio. An employer needs to not only know if you have the ability to design but also can comprehend the technical aspect of the job. A technical sketch should include specific details about how to construct the garment if it were to go into production. The sketch should have important measurements, detailed seaming and stitching that will help communicate in a more comprehensive aspect what the garment should look like. *(Figure 4-2)*

## Fashion Illustrations

Following these Mini-Collections, you should also include several pages with individual fashion illustrations or sketches with the front and back of a design. Along with these sketches you should always have the corresponding flat sketch, demonstrating your knowledge of construction. *(Figure 4-3)*

## Don't Date Your Sketches

A great piece of advice I was once given about my portfolio was to never put a date on your sketches. When creating my groupings or individual illustrations, I would often categorize them by season: "Spring 2017" or "Fall 2018." What happens is that soon your sketches become "dated" themselves. Pun intended! After a few interviews, you will pull out your portfolio and realize that you are suddenly out of style; which is the worst thing to be in the fashion industry. Keep any identifying markings, such as dates and seasons, off your sketches and your portfolio will become much more timeless and allow you to not constantly feel the need to update it.

## Fill Every Page

In terms of your portfolio, fill every page. You don't want the interviewer to be flipping through your book and suddenly come across 20 empty portfolio sleeves. I also prefer to see sketches on the front and back of the page, but that is often a personal choice.

## Don't Clutter the Pages

Keep each page clean, neat and not too busy. Skip the glitter and flora and fauna. Let your work speak for itself.

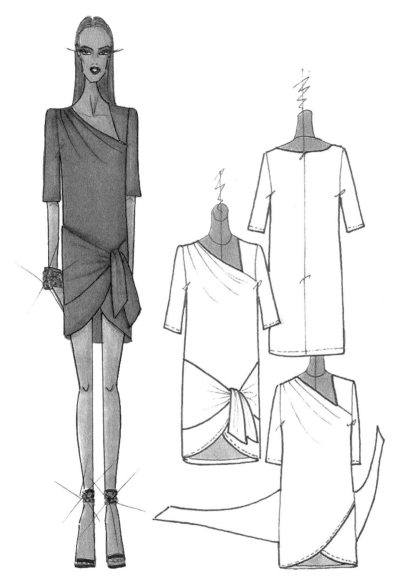

**Figure 4-3:** Fashion Illustration with corresponding Flat Sketches

## Customize Your Portfolio

It is important to keep in mind the company that you will be interviewing with and if possible, customize your portfolio to reflect the corresponding "market" that reflects that design company.

When I was a fashion design student, I was very interested in high fashion and couture. Gianni Versace, Yves Saint Laurent and Valentino were my idols and most of my sketches reflected this. There were no jeans and t-shirt fashion illustrations included in my portfolio, just pages and pages of UBER elaborate gowns and cocktail dresses. My portfolio was ideal if I were interviewing for the job of Beyonce's designer for the Met Ball, but not for an assistant design position at Nike or Forever 21, which was more in line with what jobs are available in real life.

So, time after time, I went on interviews at sportswear companies that made basic t-shirts and jeans, but I was showing my interviewers my portfolio filled with couture gowns. After several appointments, one interviewer finally told me that my portfolio was outstanding and I obviously was very talented but (here comes the "but") that I was "over-qualified." I quickly got the point and went back home to retool my portfolio. As soon as I got the call from the FIDM career center telling me that there was another job prospect, I asked for the name of the company and if there were any details on what kind of fashion they made. I then went on to customize my portfolio to include sketches that were more in line with the type of company I was interviewing with. I still kept some of those fabulous "Nick Verreos Couture" gown sketches, but I added some illustrations of basic sportswear that would reflect the type of designer the employer was looking to hire. In case you're wondering, it worked. I got the jobs each and every time.

## Should I Add Photos of My Designs in My Portfolio?

As a recent fashion school graduate, it definitely adds a boost to your portfolio when you are able to add professional photos alongside your sketches. Because I was in the exclusive Advanced Fashion Design program when I graduated from school, I was lucky enough to have beautiful runway photos of my 10-piece collection. I would place these gorgeous photos alongside my sketches, and I would inevitably get "Oohs and Aahs" when I opened my portfolio.

With that being said, you must be very careful and judicious when deciding whether or not a photo enhances your portfolio or detracts from the overall impression you are trying to relay. The photos I had were of professional models on the runway or in a photoshoot. If you are lucky enough to collaborate with a fantastic photographer or if you also have high quality images from your graduating collection, then it is an absolute MUST to include them in your selection. But, unfortunately, this is not always available to young designers that are just starting out in the workplace. Often, a nice substitute for a professional image would be to take a photo of your design on a dress form with a clean professional studio-like backdrop. By doing this, no one will judge your model or styling decisions. The important thing is to make it look clean, chic and presentable.

## Do You Add Press Clippings?

When it comes to press clippings and whether or not to include them in your portfolio, the consensus among most professionals tends to be "no." Instead, many suggest to have a separate folder for press clippings that also often include the photos which I was describing above.

When I began interviewing, I have to admit that I DID include press clippings. I was just happy to have any press and naturally wanted to include it. But I soon realized that it was a bit too much and slightly "self-branding," especially for an entry level design job.

Your main portfolio should be about your designs, sketches and inspiration. Your goal is to show your prospective boss that you have the design acumen for that specific job. Adding press clippings can disrupt your portfolio and take away from what is most important. But, if you have a separate folder or smaller book with press clippings and photos, you should have it on hand just in case you are asked or if you find it appropriate to present.

## What Not to Include in Your Portfolio

I advise everyone to stay away from art sketches and art renderings. These sketches don't really have anything to do with fashion. These types of drawings are fine if you are applying for an assistant position with an artist or painter, but otherwise stick to fashion illustrations. Obviously, if you are applying for a position as a textile designer or graphic designer, any work that you have done to create textiles or artwork is a MUST to add to your portfolio.

## CHAPTER 5

# Starting a Career in Fashion

Starting a career in fashion can take many different routes for many different people. Because there are so many jobs in the fashion industry, it becomes easy to see how someone can transition from one type of job to another, all within the same industry, throughout their career.

This is basically what happened to me. Fresh out of fashion school, one can have a vision or goal of what they want to do or where they want to be, but as they say . . . you never know where you might end up. My road to a career in fashion took several different avenues, but in the end all those avenues and everything I learned converged into one "Grand Boulevard" that really defined, and continues to define, my passion for fashion. I want to share my personal experience in starting a career in fashion as a way to illustrate the many different opportunities one may encounter in achieving a worthwhile—and fashionable—career.

## My First Job

One could make a good case that my entry into the fashion industry really began when I was sixteen years old with my mom driving me to

91

the local Macy's, whereupon I got my first paid job as a Sales Associate. But in truth, it really wasn't until many years later when I answered an ad to be an intern for a Fashion Company while attending FIDM.

I was heading into my final year at school and beginning to think about employment in the industry and a life outside of the secure campus walls. I, once again, visited my trusty Career Center and while looking past the typical notices for Fashion Show Dressers, something else caught my interest. There was a post stating "Assistant needed for a Fashion Designer in West Hollywood." The job was entry level; no previous experience needed and was listed by an FIDM alumni. I rode my little scooter to the corner of Santa Monica and Fairfax Avenue and proceeded to walk up the flight of stairs leading to a cavernous hallway. I knocked on the door and was greeted by James Clay, who would be my first "fashion career" employer and mentor. Clay was a fashion and costume designer who created custom garments for private clientele which included several famous celebrities.

My eyes widened with sheer joy when he told me that he was busy working on an outfit for actress Delta Burke of "Designing Women" (remember this was the 1990s so don't judge!). In the office of his atelier, we went through the normal interview protocol. I showed him my sketches and I told him about the Debut Collection I was working on back at FIDM. He told me of my duties, which would be assisting in his workroom with little things here and there; sketching flats, cutting fabric and all the basics of an entry level job in fashion.

Happily, the interview went well and I got the job. I was to return several days later to start. Bright eyed and bushytailed, I was ready for my first day in becoming Fashion Fabulous. Or so I thought: My first day on the job, almost became my last.

## Stay Humble

I now had my first job, I was working on my graduate collection at FIDM and basically feeling quite confident in myself. I was ready to tackle the world and felt I could handle anything someone threw at me. But soon reality would give me a swift slap across the face. Only minutes after walking into my new place of employment on my first day, my boss gave me a test. It wasn't your average type of test with written questions or multiple choice answers. This was a Fashion Industry test. Uh oh . . ..

I should backtrack a little bit and say that I didn't realize at the time that he was testing me; I just thought this was my first on-the-job duty. I was to cut fabric for a client's new design. Clay took out a bolt of black silk chiffon fabric and gave me a pattern for a long maxi skirt. He told me that he needed me to cut these patterns out of the chiffon. He told me the silk chiffon was very expensive and from France. In other words: Don't be wasteful when cutting it. "Perfect!" I thought, "Will do!" I said. This sounds easy-breezy enough. He then left the workroom to attend to his appointments and the daily grind of running a design business, leaving me alone at a cutting table to do my job.

I spread the tissue-thin, fragile silk chiffon fabric across the table and then placed the pattern pieces on top of the fabric. I proceeded to delicately pin the fabric to the pattern using small straight pins. I cannot be dramatic enough when I try and recount to you what happened next: As I began cutting, the fabric kept slipping and sliding with every attempt I made at cutting. I continued trying to cut, while somehow attempting to manipulate the fabric with my hands. I finished the first piece, took out the pins, lifted the pattern paper and what should have looked like the front of a skirt, resembled something more similar to a jig saw puzzle piece. So, I did it again. Same result. And again, with the same results each time.

At this point, I was using what looked like hundreds of pins in an attempt to stabilize the expensive silk chiffon fabric and prevent it from shifting and swerving. By now, I had already wasted several yards of fabric and there wasn't much left. Not to mention the fact that it had been at least an hour and a half since I started this seemingly simple task. I was sweating, frustrated and felt as if my heart was racing a mile a minute. How could I mess up the first duty on my first day on the job? I began to wonder if my first day in the fashion industry might be my last. Suddenly, my boss of only one day, walked into the quiet workroom and incredulously asked why I was still cutting that same pattern and why I wasn't done. I looked up at him like a little puppy who had just had an accident on the carpet.

I began explaining how I repeatedly tried to cut the silk chiffon and each attempt resulted in very pathetic results. He quietly but firmly reprimanded me for not only being wasteful with the fabric but also with my time. He exclaimed that if this were a production garment being produced by a larger company I would most likely have been fired on the spot. Luckily for me, Clay calmly proceeded to show me the proper way to cut this very delicate fabric. He effortlessly rolled the chiffon fabric atop a thin brown layer of paper. On top of both of those two pieces he pinned the pattern through all three layers. He handed me the scissors and had me cut through all of them. Within 5 minutes, I had beautifully cut out the entire skirt. I'm pretty sure I shook uncontrollably with both joy and bemusement at the fact that it was so simple.

Clay later told me that the whole thing was a test, and while I failed miserably in the task, he saw something in my spirit and willingness to learn that thankfully saved my job. Most importantly I learned from the experience that you can never be too confident and expect that just by having a solid education, you know everything about the business. After 20 years in the fashion industry I continue to learn something new almost every day.

## Jobs, Jobs, Jobs

Following graduation, I went on many interviews for entry-level positions within the Southern California fashion industry. For a brief time, I thought about possibly leaving Los Angeles for New York to look for jobs after graduation. But quite frankly, I didn't feel like I had the money or chutzpah to get up and leave everything I had in Los Angeles. Since it was so important for me to find employment right away, I looked at every option available to me in the industry and took every job that I could get. I have since found that this is quite common among graduates in fashion. Often, the path that you have mapped out for your life, is not always achieved in the direct course that you had intended.

One of the scariest parts of graduating from college is finding employment; not to mention a job in a career that you actually aspire to work in for decades to come. My advice is to have no fear (or at least try to convince yourself to have no fear). You must attack the task as fervently and with as much passion as you would tackle a design project. You mustn't let yourself get frustrated and you need to continue to pursue every opportunity available to you. For me, I continually "stalked" the Career Center and I was also an avid follower of the *California Apparel News*. The *Apparel News* was, and continues to be, the leading Southern California fashion industry trade publication. Consider it the *WWD* of the West Coast. And more importantly for me, they have a fantastic classified ads section in the back of the paper advertising jobs that range from assistant designer to patternmaker and everything in between. It certainly was my "Job Bible" for a while.

# Buying Office

One of my first jobs in the industry was a brief stint in a fashion buying office at the California Mart in Downtown LA. I did it because it was a job and they paid, but I hated it. Well, maybe "hated" is too strong of a word; I was just disinterested and didn't feel challenged or motivated there. First off, I wasn't designing or working in an exciting design room and as a creative type; I felt as if I was wasting my time. Besides that, I really disliked sitting at a desk filing orders and watching sales rep's do their selling "shtick" to store buyers. I think I probably lasted a couple of months at that particular job until an actual design room position came along.

When I worked in this fashion buying showroom, I thought that my time there was not really beneficial to my overall path to becoming a fashion designer or at the very least, getting started in a career in fashion. It would not be an understatement to say that I was very naïve about these feelings. I say this now because I have since learned that one of the most important aspects of my career as a designer is to sell my clothing. Once I started my own company, I realized that the time I spent in that showroom watching the sales representatives selling the garments, was one of the most beneficial lessons I could learn. After forming my own company and creating collections for many years now, I have had to sell and present my vision to store buyers all across the country and even throughout the entire world. And, little did I know, that very underappreciated job in a showroom would one day help me in my ability to work on television and present my clothing line to millions of women on a shopping network. I learned that I needed to be, not only passionate about the design process, but also enthusiastic about how I described and spoke about my collections.

That first job, like most of the other small jobs I embarked on in the industry, taught me a lesson and enriched my path. It molded me into becoming a well-rounded and knowledgeable fashion designer and taught me to embrace every job with the understanding that even the smallest tasks can be a teachable moment.

## Design Assistant

When I began my career in fashion, Southern California was on its way to becoming the nucleus of Junior Sportswear. This type of clothing that is generally designed for teenagers and twenty-somethings, is cheap, trendy and quick to produce. While there were a few design companies in Los Angeles doing what is considered High Fashion, the majority of those companies are located on the East Coast or in Europe.

So, for my first years working in the fashion industry, my employment was mainly as a design assistant in Junior clothing companies. The nature of these jobs would be more akin to what we now call internships. As most entry level positions require, I was responsible for all the menial tasks in the design room. I would get the coffee, pick up fabric and sweep the floors, cut samples, and even tear out pages from a fashion magazine. These "tear sheets" would often be the way these companies "designed" their clothing. I would then re-draw the garments from the magazine so that they were less high fashion and more fast-fashion. Also, it was necessary to change them enough so that it wouldn't look as if the company was directly "knocking off" the garment. As harsh at it sounds, this was (and still is) a major component of the fashion industry. And it has become even more so with the advent of "fast fashion" retailers and fashion brands such as Forever 21, H&M, Zara, ASOS, and so on. With that said, I was happy to be employed and thrilled to be getting a paycheck. I remember these entry level design jobs paid about $400 a week, which I was very excited to be getting. No more calls to my mom and dad asking them to deposit more money in my bank account!

# After Work Passion

Even though cutting swatches and tracing designs might not have seemed like the ideal fashion job, I knew that I had to start somewhere. I was happy to have a job and be financially independent. However, I felt a bit stunted in my creativity and sensed that I was slowly losing touch with my aspirations. Instead of whining and complaining about not really designing at my day job, I decided that I would do something about it. I began to make my own creations at home. After a long day at work, I would drive back to my apartment and start working on my designs in my newly created workroom. Much to my roommate's dismay, I had fashioned a nice little design studio out of our dining room, complete with pattern table, dress forms, sewing machine and racks. I now had my very own fashion "man cave."

For several years, I would come home from work, have my dinner and then walk to my "atelier" and create a design from sketch to drape to pattern to sewn garment. This also became a great "Fashion School: Part Two" for me. I schooled myself in patternmaking and draping by trial and error and without the horror of having to be graded by an instructor. I went through my fashion school patternmaking book from cover to cover; all 500+ pages and studied it like it was THE BIBLE. I did many of the exercises in the draping and pattern books without the fear or time constraints of a school assignment. I wanted to almost re-teach myself. And I did.

As a result of my post–9-to-5 secret life, I designed and made enough garments to almost have a complete collection. I even crafted my own "Nick Verreos" label. When I heard through the grapevine that someone was putting on a fashion show and needed designers, I would be there with my post–9-to-5 "collection." On some of the more intricate and fabulous designs, I even began seeking the sewing aid of a former FIDM classmate of mine and also from a seamstress that I befriended at work. As it turns out, I wasn't the only one moonlighting after work! Both women continued to teach me so much about construction and sewing and how to make my patterns better and more efficient.

During one of these fashion shows in which I participated, I became friends with a fellow designer. He was a big help to me during late night crunch hours when my Singer sewing machine wouldn't do the job. He had several industrial machines and was kind enough to let me use his studio as my own. I soon learned that while my day job was a lowly $400 per week, he worked as a $900 per week Patternmaker.

# Me . . . A Patternmaker?

After one late night design room marathon, my patternmaker-by-day/designer-by-night buddy, told me that he was leaving his job to go to work at another design company that was offering more money. He knew that I was not content at my job picking up fabric off the floor and flat sketching someone else's ideas, and that I had a desire to move on. He suggested that I try and apply for his job . . . as a Pattern-maker. At first I wondered if he had lost his mind and was on some medication that had subsequently made his brain a bit woozy. But no, he was serious. Many thoughts began racing through my head. Mainly, the fact that I felt like I was a Fashion Designer and not a Patternmaker, and that I really didn't focus on all the technical aspect of construction and design when I was attending school. In fact, I remember disliking my pattern classes immensely! In addition, I assumed you would need years of on-the-job training to be hired in a position like his.

He shut all my objections down with the following arguments: He first told me that he was quite sure that I could do his job, pointing to the fact that I'd been making my own patterns while creating my post-work secret collections. Secondly, he said, it would make me TWICE the salary. Now that was a really good point! Ultimately, he also argued that I would be creating garments on a daily basis. Although they might be someone else's designs, I would still be much more involved in the design process.

# Fudging the Truth

Since I live by a "No Should've Would've Could've: Just Do It!" policy, I decide why not go for it and give it a try. What did I have to lose? So, with that decision made, I embarked on something that I do not condone: fudge the truth to get a job. Before calling the company inquiring about the newly-opened Patternmaking position, I first had to create a resume mentioning that I had been a Patternmaker for other companies (Truth-fudging No. 1) and that I had 5+ years of experience as the aforementioned Patternmaker (Truth-fudging No. 2).

In my "new and improved" resume, I stated that I was a Patternmaker for James Clay Atelier. I didn't really lie since during my time interning with Clay, I did make some patterns. I also added that I did patterns for a certain David Paul. David happened to be my boyfriend who was getting his Master's Degree in Costume Design at UCLA and in fact, I did create the patterns for some of his fabulous costumes for various operas and theater productions. Finally, I added that I was the Patternmaker for my own design company that didn't really exist. These "jobs" added up to about 5 years, so in actuality I wasn't really exaggerating on that front, if you were to believe my job titles. So, now with my resume re-done, I was ready to tackle a new opportunity and unbeknownst to me, enter a new phase of my design career.

# Test No. 2

I arrived to my interview ready to show my stuff! I brought my trusty Tool Kit with my rulers, shears and pattern blocks (base patterns used to make other patterns). I also had my new resume. The head designer of the company greeted me and I gave her my resume—which she barely looked at—thank goodness! She was less interested in who I had worked for and more concerned about whether or not I could actually make a pattern. She showed me to an empty pattern table in the sewing room and then gave me a photo of a woman's jacket. She then proceeded to tell me that this was a test (Oh no! Not another test!), and I was to make the pattern for the jacket in the photo.

In a hot minute, I went from looking and acting like the coolest fashion cat in the room to a sweating, nervous know-nothing. After briefly and privately freaking out, I gathered my senses and went for it. I breathed slowly and just said to myself "pretend you're at home and making a pattern for one of your own designs." The difference was that there were about ten Latina ladies seated in front of their sewing machines staring at me as if I was an endangered white tiger. Also, it didn't help that they were all talking about me. I knew this because I speak fluent Spanish. They, of course, didn't realize I spoke Spanish. The sewing ladies weren't being mean but they were just wondering who I was and why such a young and stylish man wanted to apply for this patternmaking position.

It took me way too long to finish my jacket pattern. Even I knew I was taking much longer than I should. Time is of the essence in big fashion companies and I was aware that Patternmakers were expected to churn out 4 to 5 (if not more) patterns a day. So far I had been at that table more than 3 hours nervously trying to finish one jacket. At this rate, I would be lucky to finish 3 patterns in a day! I really hoped that the designer wasn't looking at the clock.

I finally finished, handed the pattern to my potential employer, wiped the sweat off my forehead, and gathered my tools. I was then told that she would call me the following day after the seamstress had created the jacket from the pattern I had just made. I quietly laughed to myself and muttered "Good Luck!" I just had a feeling that it would be a sunny day in London if any of my patterns actually worked.

That night I went home under no illusion that I would be getting the job. But hey, "at least I tried," I told myself. The following day, I received a call: It was the designer. She said "Hi Nick!" and followed it quickly with "You got the job! The jacket turned out great!" I was floored, to say the least. I think I might have even said "Really? It actually worked?!" (I need to keep my Loud Voice in check!) She then asked if "$900 per week is OK?" When she said that, I almost screamed, but then I regained my composure and replied "Yes, it's perfectly fine."

For the next seven years, I was a Patternmaker. I worked for that initial company for several years until I was eventually poached away by other companies. In time, I made somewhat of a name for myself within the patternmaking mini-world. All I could think about was the fact that my patternmaking instructors would never in a million years think that I would become a highly sought after Patternmaker in some of Southern California's top "fast-fashion" companies.

## Freelance Years

Because I remained a designer at heart, having my regular 9-to-5 Patternmaking job just wasn't enough. I needed to push myself further. I soon began taking on side jobs and doing freelance patterns for start-up designers as well as other major design companies. I would consistently get calls from people saying that someone had recommended me as a good patternmaker and that they needed five dress styles made, or a pattern for a pair of jeans, etc. It was great extra cash as well. I charged $200 for a pair of jeans, $250 for a jacket, $100 for a blouse, and $50+ for a basic t-shirt. One client wanted me to create their entire ten-piece dress line, from patterns to samples, and I did. Most of these jobs came from recommendations and referrals. I became friends with several other Southern California freelance patternmakers and when they were too busy with the jobs they'd taken, they would refer me to their clients as well.

I also began taking on other jobs that involved designing as well as fashion illustrating. I designed and did the patterns for several boutiques as well as manufacturers who sold and shipped to stores across the country. I also was contacted by designers who would hire me to draw fashion illustrations of their designs that could then be used for publicity purposes or pitching a design project.

My freelance jobs became so lucrative, in fact, that I gave up my day job and began working from home. My dining room now truly was my official Design Studio and because I could make my own hours and work from home, I also had the added luxury of continuing to design and create more of my own ideas. Slowly, I became more confident in my designs and began the transition to creating custom garments and eventually my own ready-to-wear collection.

## Pageant Fab

Through word of mouth or perhaps after seeing my designs at various fashion shows, I also began gaining private clients. I was soon making designs for various models, actresses and especially beauty pageant winners. My sister, Rita, was a former Miss Venezuela contestant back in 1988. Soon after, she also moved to Los Angeles to pursue her studies at UCLA and seek a career in Hollywood. It became a wonderful way for me to dress someone in my newly created designs for whatever event or function she was invited to attend and have a real-life "Barbie" to play dress up with.

I was also contacted by the Miss Universe organization which was based out of Los Angeles back then. Someone had given them my name as a designer who was known to make Evening Gowns. I had India's first-ever Miss Universe, Sushmita Sen, wear several of my dresses and I also designed and made a very sexy gown for Ali Landry, who was Miss USA 1996.

Ali was giving up her crown and wanted to "go out with a bang!" The base of the gown I created was made from a black illusion material with sequined lace appliqués covering all the important areas. Along with David and our Seamstress Extraordinaire, Wendy, we spent 100+ hours strategically hand-sewing the appliqués onto the base using a dress form as a guide of what areas to properly cover. Once it was done, she came in for a final fitting and looked absolutely stunning. Very risqué for 1997, but boy did she look HOT!

Many years later, I had the pleasure of working with Ali Landry at TV Guide Network where we were covering the Red Carpet for the Academy Awards. We reminisced on that time when I made her the very risqué gown. She shared with me that she was almost banned from wearing the dress but she was defiant and wore it in spite of the objections! You go girl! It was an absolute thrill to see Ali in my gown on national TV, as millions and millions of viewers were watching. After that experience I went on to make gowns for several other Pageant contestants including Miss Universe, Miss USA, and Miss California.

# The Birth of Nikolaki

After almost a decade of working in the fashion industry in various job positions, I came across an opportunity that I could not pass up. I discovered that the iconic Manhattan department store, Henri

Sashes and Tiaras: original sketch of Miss USA Ali Landry in NIKOLAKI

Bendel, was coming to Los Angeles for the very first time. They were scouting the West Coast for brands and designers that they might potentially carry in their flagship Manhattan store. Besides being known for their upscale designer brands and fabulous gift boxes and wrapping, Henri Bendel was also famous for having their "Open-See

The Birth of NIKOLAKI: Henri Bendel Dresses

Casting Call" once a year. On these special days, Bendel's would give new designers a once-in-a-lifetime chance to present their designs and possibly have the buyers place an order and carry the brand in their store. It was like a *Project Runway* audition, but for retail.

So you can imagine the incredible buzz this received in Southern California when word got out that Henri Bendel was coming to town. Naturally, I wanted to be there. I gathered about ten of my designs and I also made an additional group of dresses using a colorful 60s vintage polka dot printed fabric I found at a local fabric store. The event was being held at a very hip hotel in Hollywood and upon arrival I dutifully joined the 400+ line of hopeful fashionistas to show my line to the very important buyers.

When it was finally my turn, I took a deep breath and put on my "Nick Show." I suddenly had flashbacks to my time working in that LA Showroom and desperately tried to remember some of the tricks the Sales Reps used when selling their clothing to stores. I showed the buyers my very elegant silk gowns and sequined one-shoulder column dresses, which I thought would hang perfectly next to any Oscar de la Renta or Carolina Herrera design. While the buyers thought they were beautiful and quite nice, they weren't interested. They stated that they had no more room in their Evening Wear Department and that they were fine with the brands they were already carrying. When they said that, I felt as if the air had been sucked out of the room and I was ready to walk out with my tail between my legs. But then, one of the buyers asked to see the other dresses; the short day dresses in the one-of-a-kind vintage polka dot fabric. I had several styles—a button-front, tie-neck shirt dress, and a backless bias-cut cowl neck design. They loved them and instantly wrote up an order for me to have delivered for the next Spring Season!

This became the beginning of **NIKOLAKI**, the design company which my partner David and I began the day after that fateful Henri Bendel meeting. It also became the beginning of my new career, finally designing my very own line.

# Nick Tips

So what did I learn throughout my personal journey from fashion school graduation until I started my own fashion business? A LOT! While everyone will have their own voyage through the trials and tribulations of the fashion world, I can hopefully make it a bit easier by sharing a few of my personal "Nick Tips." With some luck, my advice will assist and guide you to a life in fashion and eventually a long and successful career.

## Start Early!

At the age of 16 as a Junior in High School, I landed my first job ever. I began working at Macy's as a Sales Associate near my home at the San Mateo Hillsdale Mall. I worked as a "floater" and went from department to department, wherever I was needed. As a young man who had a secret "passion for fashion," it was a nice way to just be amongst all the beautiful clothing. Because I was a young guy, my manager would put me in the "Men's Furnishings" section. While I was fine working amongst the ties and belts, all I really wanted to do was be near the Women's Clothing Department. At that time, it was a big no-no to have a man work in the women's department, much less a 16-year old boy. But I am sure I probably would have been fabulous at selling sequined Mother-of-the-Bride dresses in the "After Five" section.

Even though I wasn't near those dresses, I was just happy to be working in the clothing business in one form or another. My retail experience didn't end in high school. After I moved to Los Angeles to attend UCLA, I also got a part-time job working at—you guessed it—a department store. This time it was Bullock's. So, even though I was studying International Relations and Political Science, I was fulfilling my love of fashion by working a few days a week amongst gorgeous clothing. And this is all before I decided to attend FIDM and fulfill my dreams of becoming a fashion designer.

The point of this story is to let you know that you should expose yourself to fashion as young as possible. It isn't important what the job might be, but it should be something that teaches you and helps you understand a little bit more about the industry you might eventually want a career in. When I needed to get a summer job during that time, it would have never occurred to me to try and get a job at McDonald's or the local coffee shop. No way! It had to be somewhere or something that was related to clothing. I didn't realize it then, but many years later, that experience helped me to sell my own clothing line to buyers and stores and to women across the world on television. Besides teaching me responsibility, time management and exposing me to how nice it is to get a paycheck and have my own money, working in a department store gave me a hands-on education in sales, dealing with clients, and learning about fabrics, silhouettes and price points. All of which would later be essential elements in my own fashion business.

## Internships

Internships are usually non-paid, part-time positions available to students still in school and even following your graduation. It has become THE NUMBER ONE way of getting your foot in the door in the fashion industry. It also allows you to utilize your skills and design talents, while also providing real-world experience. Internships usually last for a short period of time. This can range from one month, a summer or sometimes even an entire year. Depending on your employer and how wonderful and valuable of an intern you have been, an internship can eventually materialize into a full-time position.

Internships in the fashion industry have also become a way in which employers test out possible candidates to work in their design company. When I graduated from fashion school, internships were not the norm as a first job. We were called Assistant Designer or just plain Assistant, and back then, we were paid for these "Internships." The word "Assistant" has now become "Intern" and paid employee has most commonly been changed to unpaid intern.

Why the change, you may ask? The reason I hear most from fashion companies, is that there is now too much risk involved. The consensus seems to be that there is a combination between a lack of loyalty and a drop in work ethic. In other words, it seems as if many recent graduates are not as interested in doing the menial tasks and are concerned more about obtaining only a higher level position.

Non-paid internships have now become "try-outs" for new hires, especially for fresh-out-of-fashion school entry level positions. No employer wants to go through the whole process of hiring an Assistant Designer outright, only to have the new employee jump ship a week later. In other words, will they do the dirty work that is essential as a new hire in the fashion industry? I know that all this sounds harsh, but this has become the reality in the business. I tell everyone this only to stress the fact that it is essential to work hard and be proactive. So, if you do land an internship, prove those fashion executives wrong and get the coffee. . . .

## Get the Coffee

Yes, get the coffee! Now, when I say those words I mean much more. In my many travels and appearances, while giving lectures at universities and to young students across the country, someone inevitably raises their hand and asks me for that one nugget of advice that will give them an advantage when starting out in the fashion industry. I can only come up with three simple words: Get the coffee.

When I say "get the coffee," yes, I do mean be willing to actually get the coffee. But what I really mean is to be ready to do EVERYTHING. Tackle every task that is thrown your way and go above and beyond what is asked of you, especially if you are just starting out and this is your first job in the industry. I did. I might not have liked or enjoyed it, but something in me knew that while I might have wished I was somewhere else or even creating my own designs, I had to pay my dues. I remember many years, especially during the busy buying season, when my bosses would request—no, actually tell me!—that I had to work on a Saturday or even Christmas Eve.

Every single successful person I know working in this industry (and many others), got the coffee. In other words, they did everything and anything that was asked of them.

## Never Say Never

A great piece of advice for students who are about to graduate from fashion school and begin their career in the industry is also to Never Say Never. I think this is certainly one of the biggest lessons which I can impart to you.

I have learned the "Never Say Never" rule throughout my career beginning very early on. Remember when I almost dismissed the whole "being a patternmaker" thing, thinking this didn't seem like the right path for me to become a successful fashion designer? Luckily, I quickly thought "why not?" and realized that there are different roads to achieve your ultimate goal.

I believe in never saying never to all the different opportunities that may come your way. If you are still at school and an internship with a Buying Office comes up, take it! (I did.) You will learn sales techniques and how to merchandise a line. If an opportunity arises for you to work backstage or in the "front of the house" at Fashion Week, take it (I did). You will get on-the-job training on how to run a fashion show. And yes, if in fact you are offered a position as a patternmaker, try it! And like me, when you eventually start your own line of clothing and need to create all the patterns for your collection, you will have saved thousands of dollars because . . . YOU DID THEM!

I hope by now you see where I am going with this golden rule: The "Never Say Never" mantra is the perfect way to motivate yourself to experience different types of jobs in the fashion industry and see which one is a good fit for you.

In your path to fashion success, it will be to your advantage to explore all your options and broaden your job universe by trying on as many "Fashion Career Hats" as possible until you find the one that fits.

# CHAPTER 6

# Careers in Fashion— A Glossary

I have put together a list of jobs within the fashion industry to help you get a feel for what these jobs are and what companies require regarding these positions. As you may know, there are many, many different types of opportunities in the wide-ranging world of fashion, so I've just compiled a basic list to help you understand the business and maybe help you get a feel for which occupation might be right for you.

## Fashion Designer

A fashion designer's job is naturally at the top of the list as one of the most desired careers in the industry. Through history, the job has been very self-explanatory: fashion designers design. Although, depending on the type of company you work for, a fashion designer is also expected to do much more.

Among their many duties, a fashion designer also studies trends, oversees the designing of collections, sketches the designs, or directs their assistants to sketch ideas for them to approve. They also are often required to do garment costing or at least be very attentive to the cost of the garments they design.

Many fashion designers—myself included—also drape their designs and might even work on the patterns that will eventually be cut and sewn into a finished toile or sample. A fashion designer should really have a mastery of all disciplines that involve the creation of a garment. Most often, if you are in a small company or beginning your own business, you will need to do more than one job as a designer. And as I stated above, the job of a fashion designer varies depending on the company as well as the size of these businesses. The fashion designer in a smaller company probably tends to be more hands on as opposed to a designer within a larger business. When I started my own design company, NIKOLAKI, along with my partner David, we both had to play many roles. Even though we both considered ourselves fashion designers, we each shared responsibility for the sketching of the collections and coming up with the design ideas; I draped the designs, while David would then cut the muslin (sample fabric) and subsequently sew the first samples.

Jobs in the industry for a fashion designer usually require years of experience, especially if you are applying to a larger fashion company. Also, many times, someone can be promoted into the design role after years and years of working as an Assistant. This is especially true if you have been with a specific company for many years and there arrives a chance to move your way up the fashion career ladder.

In many of the larger, conglomerate fashion companies that are comprised of different divisions, there is also the likelihood that there will be numerous fashion designers within the various departments. There could be a designer (or several designers) for the Children's Division, a separate one for Women's, Men's and even Maternity or Plus Size, if that is in their corporation. In addition to this, all these designers answer to someone above them, who would have the title of Senior Designer or Creative Director/Design Director.

## Assistant Designer

An Assistant Designer can be considered an entry level position within some companies but in essence, an internship is most likely your first position in the industry. If there is an opening within the design department, and you are fortunate enough to be hired in a paid position, the next level up on the design ladder would be the position of assistant designer or assistant to the designer. For the most part, as an assistant designer, the emphasis is on the word *Assistant*; you are assisting in most everything that pertains to the design process. You help in putting together mood boards, sourcing fabrics, choosing colors, and often keeping the design room organized and on schedule. You are also expected to do lots of flat sketches—on computer or by hand. As it is with most entry level design positions in the fashion industry, knowledge in Photoshop, Illustrator, Excel, and CAD (computer aided design and drafting) are all a must.

## Associate Designer

An Associate Designer is someone who collaborates with several other designers who then, subsequently, report to a more senior-level designer or creative director. A good analogy is like a law firm; you have your senior partners and your associate partners; there is a similar concept within an apparel company, especially larger businesses. Typically, to be an associate designer, you will need experience in that position for several years and all the knowledge and skills that any fashion designer should already have. You will also need to have strong people skills and be able to work as a team and within a group environment. This is not a position where you can be the single design "Diva"; remember you're an Associate Designer, so you will need to be a leader but also work collaboratively.

## Senior Designer

Speaking of Design Diva, a Senior Designer is usually at the top of the Designer "food chain" especially within a larger fashion company. As I stated before, in these larger businesses, there are usually several designers—or associate designers—and above them is a Senior Designer. The associate designers would report to this senior-level employee, as well as collaborate on the styles, silhouettes, textiles and basically the final outcome of the entire collection. A Senior Designer sets the vision for the design company's aesthetic. They also pitch these concepts to the Creative Director, who is above them in title and position. The Senior Designer manages line plans throughout the development process, establishes color palettes for new seasons, conducts fittings for development and pre-production, as well as oversees the work load of the Associate Designers. Achieving this position usually requires 5-10 years of experience, depending on the apparel companies that you are applying to.

## Creative Director/Design Director

The job of a Creative Director is to direct and manage the fashion designer(s). In addition, and more importantly, a Creative Director in a fashion company gives all the designers an inspiration, a vision/directive, to then carry out among all the departments for all the different seasons and collections. Think of a Creative Director as the CDO, Chief *Design* Officer.

A good example in recent fashion history of a "famous" Creative Director is Tom Ford when he was at the design helm of Gucci in the mid-1990s. Besides being the face of the newly-rebranded iconic Italian fashion and leather goods empire, his position was to be in charge of all the different design departments—womenswear, menswear, accessories, handbags, shoes, jewelry, and even the design of the stores. All the designers in each of those departments would report to him. Ford would oversee what each department was working on as well as designing and in the end, be accountable for each and every product. Other prominent examples of Creative Directors in the fashion industry are Raf Simons when he was at Christian Dior, Karl Lagerfeld at Chanel, and Miuccia Prada for her own eponymous line.

## Technical Designer

A Technical Designer is one of the most senior positions within the production and pre-production end of an apparel company. Even though the word *designer* is in the title, the more important part is the *Technical*; they aid in the design of the garments, but more from the technical aspect. Because of that, a Technical Designer must have patternmaking knowledge, be able to conduct fittings, generate fit comments, and have an extensive knowledge of garment construction. Besides the patternmaker, they are the contact person who can tell the Associate Designers and/or Senior Designers, what they can or cannot do in regards to their design. In other words, they can point out to a designer if a certain garment they have envisioned can be achieved within the constraints of sewing, pattern, textiles, etc. They are also a liaison with the factories as well as the sewing and pattern room.

# Production Assistant

A Production Assistant is an assistant position that deals specifically with the production end of the garment as opposed to the first sample. In other words, a Production Assistant's duties deal more with creating tech packs, technical sketches, and all the production components that go into creating a garment. They are, more often than not, in contact with the local and/or overseas factories, facilitating the manufacturing of the final production of the garments and may work under or alongside a Technical Designer. This is a job that is more heavily involved with the post-design process.

# Textile Designer

Many fashion companies pride themselves on creating their own fabrics that are exclusive to their business. A Textile Designer is in charge of designing and creating these textiles. This is especially important when creating unique prints and patterns for each new season. They work with the company's design staff and collaborate in creating the right textile vision for each season. A Textile Designer's position is not just exclusive to fashion companies, as many independent fabric manufacturers employ Textile Designers to create their distinct fabrics for mass production. People who are interested and have a passion for fabrics, textiles and graphic design are ideal for this position.

# Patternmaker

A patternmaker creates the patterns for the construction of the clothing. It is a very important step in the design and creative process and can often times change the eventual outcome of the design. This is how it usually works: The fashion designer and/or assistant designer of an apparel company gives sketches of their designs to a patternmaker. These are usually flat sketches but could also be quick sketches. It is then the job of the patternmaker to create a paper pattern, either from a discipline called flat patterning or by draping. After the patterns are done, they are given to the cutter who uses the pattern to cut the fabric, and then to the sewer to actually create the final product. The patternmaker can create the pattern by drafting on a flat surface from measurements using curved and straight rulers or use fabric to drape the design on a dress form before transferring it to dotted paper. The ability to do both methods is definitely an asset to any patternmaker, but the skill to drape is especially important if you are applying for a position in a high-end, more Couture-like fashion company. It is also important for the patternmaker to have good knowledge of sketching, particularly flat or technical sketching. Even if a designer has handed you a certain drawing, the patternmaker might need to convey, through their own sketch, all the changes that had to be implemented.

The job of a patternmaker requires quite a bit of technical knowledge, but they should also have a keen eye for design. Often a patternmaker will change the shape of a garment to accommodate fabric yardage, or the width of a collar or sleeve to make it more visually pleasing or even cost effective.

A fundamental knowledge of math and especially working with fractions is important. You have to be someone who likes precision and can detect the difference between $1/16$" and $1/8$".

Not many people coming out of fashion school want to go into the field of patternmaking, but I highly recommend it as an option. Why? For one, it is one of the most available positions in the fashion industry. You will find that when looking for a job in the business, there seems to be an abundance of options available for working as a patternmaker. In my experience, patternmakers are usually older due to the fact that they need to have a certain level of experience and technique. But often, fashion companies are looking for younger patternmakers that may have a more modern "design eye" and understand current silhouettes and trends. This is especially important if you are working in a Contemporary or Fast-Fashion apparel company. I also feel that it is a great way to grow as a designer. It expands your technical understanding of the design process and pushes you to be more creative with the new knowledge you have gained through this technique.

With the broad title of patternmaker, the job can be divided into two positions: First Patternmaker and Production Patternmaker.

## First Patternmaker

A First Patternmaker creates the patterns for the first samples. Therefore, this person is responsible for the first "draft" of the garment that the designer has sketched and handed over to the patternmaker to create. These patterns, and eventually garments, are part of the sample collection that the design team has created to eventually sell to the stores and/or consumer. Not all of the samples from a collection are eventually put into production. Therefore, these first patterns do not necessarily have to be incredibly precise with their fit. Usually, a First Patternmaker is required to do several garments a day. For a "Fast-Fashion" apparel company, five patterns a day is normal; for a gown or more Couture-like company, one or two patterns a day—depending on the complexity of the style—would be expected. Because their job is to just create the patterns for the samples, a First Patternmaker is not responsible for the production pattern (the pattern of the garment that has been ordered and sold to a store); that job is the responsibility of a Production Patternmaker.

## Production Patternmaker

The Production Patternmaker is the person who is in charge of the Production Pattern of a garment that has been ordered by a store. When a store has ordered a certain style from the collection by looking at a particular sample, it is then the job of the Production Patternmaker to create the finished production pattern of that garment. They fix anything that needs to be adjusted from the First Pattern, which might range from a tighter fit, longer skirt or perhaps adjust the width of a collar. Corrections are made and then another sample is sewn for a production fitting with a fit model. A Production

Patternmaker is usually on hand at the fittings to make further adjustments and then eventually finalize the production pattern. As a result of these added responsibilities and importance of the final pattern needing to be PERFECT, a production patternmaker's salary is much more than a First Patternmaker and can be $100,000+ per year, after many years in the industry. With that being said, because of cost or company size, there are many businesses that combine both the First and Production Patternmaking positions into one: The title for this job would be 1st-Production Patternmaker.

## Draper/Tailor

Most mass manufacturing apparel companies do not have a separate Draper/Tailor position in their design room. As I stated previously, the patternmaker is expected to take care of these duties if needed. However, it is common for high-end, designer companies to have a Draper/Tailor whose sole responsibility is to drape the garments—especially an intricate gown—as part of the creative process of a garment. These positions are common in a workroom of a "Couture" fashion house or a design company that specializes in evening wear.

## Cutter

A cutter is responsible for laying out the pattern in a cost-effective manner on the fabric and cutting the pieces to be sewn. This person works in the workroom alongside the patternmakers and sewers. Often, in mass production, the cutter is responsible for cutting numerous garments at the same time, by stacking layers of fabric and using specialty cutting machines. This produces multiple pieces of the same garment at one time. This position doesn't necessarily require a fashion school degree, but what is more important is previous on-the-job experience cutting fabrics.

## Technical/Spec Writer

A Technical Writer creates something called specification sheets (spec packs) and technical packets (tech packs) for the garments going into production. A Technical Writer is very involved with the production end of the fashion industry. A strong knowledge of the language involved with pattern and sewing construction is key. This position can also be considered a "Technical Designer" or "Production Assistant" in some fashion career circles.

## Buyer

An Apparel Buyer is someone who places the orders from a fashion company for their seasonal collections. A buyer can work for a department store, boutique, online store or even TV Home Shopping Network. They visit the respective apparel company's showroom, survey the line and place orders accordingly. Obviously, a strong knowledge of trends, colors and fabrication is needed. Also, a buyer is responsible for finding new designers and clothing lines and is constantly needing to be aware of the "Hottest Trends." In addition to this, a very important aspect of being a Fashion Buyer is the knowledge of how to merchandise. They must be able to put together the garments in a way that will work for their respective stores and clientele.

## Fashion Illustrator

A Fashion Illustrator is an artist that specializes in drawings that focus on fashion. In the late 19th Century and the first half of the 20th Century, the job of a Fashion Illustrator was very important, especially when it came to showing the latest trends in magazines. Before the advent of modern photography, someone had to draw the current styles from Paris and London and entice women to shop. Even with the advent of photography in the 1930s, you could still find a large amount of illustrations in top magazines such as *Harper's Bazaar* and *Vogue*, but over time they began to disappear. In the 1970s there was a resurgence of Fashion Illustrations, with Antonio Lopez leading the pack with his gorgeous and stylized sketches. But, once again, the Fashion Illustrator fell out of favor and became something of a novelty, especially with the rise of digital photography.

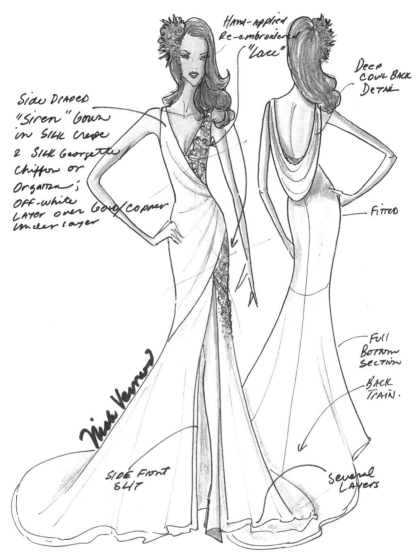

Hand-applied
Re-embroidered
"Lace"

Deep
Cowl Back
Detail

Side Draped
"Siren" Gown
in Silk Crepe
& Silk Georgette
Chiffon or
Organza;
Off-white
Layer over Gold/Copper
Under layer

Fitted

Full
Bottom
Section

Back
Train.

Side Front
Slit

Several
Layers

Nick Verreos Fashion Illustration

Slowly, we are seeing the return of illustrations. Because of social media and the need for interesting content, fashion drawings are being embraced as something that is artistic and beautiful. Many high-end fashion companies employ fashion illustrators to exclusively sketch their designs for public relations purposes. Often you will now see elaborate sketches of a wedding gown for a celebrity client or a striking illustration of a custom Haute Couture gown that was made exclusively for an actress on the Red Carpet.

For the most part a Fashion Illustrator is not a full-time position found in most apparel companies and is considered more of a freelance job. Although, it is still a very important part of the fashion world.

# Stylist

The word *styliste* in the French language basically means "A Designer." The French definition describes a *styliste* as someone who "sketches ideas and creates a fashion collection." I presume this comes from the fact that early on, the great designers such as Cristobal Balenciaga, Christian Dior and Yves Saint Laurent would not only design the clothing, but also be responsible for the hats, shoes and bags that went with each and every ensemble. And once it was time to send out the models on the catwalk, it was the fashion designers who styled the models from head to toe. In modern times, many of the high-profile designers hire fashion stylists to style their runway shows and editorial campaigns.

So what is a Stylist most commonly defined as today? A stylist is a person who chooses a wardrobe or garment that will best exemplify the entire overall look of their client and how they project themselves. Whether it is a high-profile Red Carpet event, a TV show appearance, private function, or a New York Fashion Week runway show, a stylist arranges and coordinates the clothes to be worn at such events. At the most fundamental part, they are a personal shopper and a merchandiser as well.

# History

Up until the 1990s, the word "stylist" was not even part of the fashion lexicon in America. They were best known as Personal Shoppers. Hollywood actresses would either pick out their own clothes or they had a specific Sales Associate at their favorite boutique who would recommend what they should or should not wear.

If you want to go back further, during the Golden Era of Hollywood, actresses such as Grace Kelly would enlist their favorite costume designers such as Edith Head, to dress them for the Oscars as well as other high profile events such as movie premieres. Sometimes, actresses had no choice and the Studios, whom they were contracted with, would appoint a Costume Designer to dress them for all media appearances. So, if you want to really go back into the history of the stylist, you might say that it was the Costume Designers of the Golden Era of Hollywood, that started it all.

Jump ahead to the early 1990s when Joan Rivers unleashed her unabashed humor and commentary on the Red Carpet. Quickly, it became obvious that most, if not all, of Hollywood needed sartorial help. Soon, Hollywood was awash with an endless amount of stylists, rushing to assist the stylishly-challenged starlets. European Designers weren't far behind with Giorgio Armani leading the pack, aiding the stylists and getting plenty of publicity along the way.

The job title of Stylist has evolved into being much more than just a personal shopper, although shopping is still a very important part. Nowadays, a stylist can be responsible for creating a star's persona and help in making them a style brand ambassador and style icon. Also, a stylist doesn't just work with Hollywood actors. Many "regular" people retain stylists. Yes, these people are usually wealthy, but in Hollywood standards, they just are not "famous."

If someone would have asked me several years back if it was necessary to attend fashion school in order to be a stylist, I might have answered with a resounding "No." But I have changed my tune: I now highly recommend that any young person wanting to be a stylist get a fashion education. What changed my mind? In my many years working in the industry and meeting countless stylists, I have found that the best and most accomplished stylists are the ones with a strong understanding of the fashion industry and most importantly the fundamentals of basic sewing, fabric terminology, color theory, and an overall grasp of the business of fashion. Trust me when I say, knowing these things will take you a long way as an assistant to a Stylist and eventually in your own career.

# CHAPTER 7

# Reality of the Fashion Business

S tarting a fashion business is a complex and incredibly difficult mission to accomplish. Entire books can be written about this one topic alone. So instead of trying to answer every question on the subject, I will tell you about a few of my personal experiences in the industry and outline some of the mistakes, pitfalls and of course, wonderful outcomes that I have had. The point of all this will hopefully be to have you learn something from what I have been through and help you in navigating the realities of starting your own fashion business.

## Zero to Sixty

Most designers have a desire to start their own fashion company and be in control of their own brand and style identity. Unfortunately, it is an incredibly daunting task that takes a massive amount of preparation and, most importantly, experience.

Picture this: I am fresh out of fashion school, bright eyed and bushy tailed and ready to be the "Next Fashion Star." I had just finished producing my very first "collection" for the FIDM DEBUT show and was feeling confident and excited about conquering the fashion world. Naturally, I had thoughts of immediately starting my own business. To heck with paying my dues and working for someone else in the industry, I wanted to have my own label and showcase my designs across the world. These thoughts lasted all but five minutes; I quickly came to my senses and realized just how overwhelming a task it would be.

Not too long after I finished fashion school, the "Star" designer from my graduating class started his own line. I was jealous. Boy, was I jealous. He was self-assured, talented and had connections overseas in order to quickly get his designs into production and have his clothing mass-produced in a matter of months.

Did I mention how jealous I was? I think I did. Cut to a year later, I met with some of my fellow FIDM DEBUT alum for coffee and some post-fashion school dish. I immediately asked how this certain "star designer" was doing. There was a pause and then one of my friends said, "Didn't you hear? He closed shop. He's no longer in business."

This was a definite reality check. It was at that moment that I realized that it isn't always about being the first. I came to the understanding that my desire of wanting to go from "Zero to Sixty" right after graduating was naive and that being more cautious would actually be the best approach.

My advice is to learn on someone else's dime. If having your own business is something that you really want, never give up on your dream, but take your time and gather all the information you can to make it a success. Every job and every experience you have in the fashion industry will help you make your own business better and stronger. Keep a diary or folder and fill it with information and contacts. When I was an assistant I accrued a Rolodex of textile companies, manufacturers, pattern grading businesses and more. Every single time the designer that I was assisting would have a meeting with a fabric or trim company, I would make sure to get a business card too. What could be better than earning a paycheck while at the same time gathering valuable information to help you achieve your own dreams?

Also, network amongst your own co-workers. Even though many of my assistant designer jobs did not have me interact with the sample makers, I would always make friends with all the seamstresses. Why you may ask? Because you never know when you might need their help in the future, if and when you branch out on your own. I would also befriend the scissor sharpener, the sewing machine repairman, and the fabric cutters. These people all turned out to be a great asset to me when I set up my first workroom.

# Ready, Set, Go!

So there I was, after years of experience in the industry, finally ready to start my business. As I mentioned earlier, I had heard about an "Open-See Casting Call" held by Henri Bendel in which they were looking for up-and-coming design talent. After presenting several dresses to the buyers, they absolutely loved two dress styles and wrote an order on the spot!

After popping some Champagne and celebrating the successful launch of our business, David and I realized we had a number of obstacles to overcome. I might have spent years gathering valuable information about designing and producing clothing, but I had not really focused on the business aspect of the industry. We suddenly realized that we needed to get our ducks in a row and FAST.

While there are many aspects of a business you need to master when creating your own line, below are a few of the essential items that are a MUST on any new company's list. So, sharpen your pencils because class is in session!

# What's in a Name?

A piece of advice that I received early on was to never use your own name as the title of your business. The primary reason being, if you become an enormous success and one day decide to sell your company for millions of dollars, you are in essence, selling your own name. You will no longer be able to design clothing using that name. This has happened to MANY designers including Jil Sander, John Galliano, Halston and Herve Leger, to name just a few. David and I chose the name NIKOLAKI for that very reason.

Once you have decided on the name of your business (whether or not it is your own personal name or something else) file the paperwork to have it trademarked. While you can continue to work as a business without a trademark, it is best to get the filing processed as soon as possible.

# Set the Foundation

Setting up a business can get complicated and can seem like a daunting task, but if you are organized and proactive, you will be happy that you have set the proper foundation for your business, especially as it begins to grow. In other words, the following information might get "business-y" and might go over your head, but stick with me!

# Sole Proprietor

Most young designers begin their business as a single person and therefore need to just file under the heading of Sole Proprietor.

A Sole Proprietor basically is defined as a business that is run by one individual person. There is not a legal distinction between the owner and the business. While this makes things easier for a single person start-up, there is more risk to you as an individual. If, let's say, you get into debt with a fabric company or manufacturer, these companies are allowed to go after your personal finances.

# LLC or S-Corporation

Forming an LLC (Limited Liability Corporation) or S-Corporation is the safest and most common approach to starting a business. Both are considered pass-through tax entities. Basically meaning that no taxes are paid at the business level and any profit or loss is passed through to the owner's personal tax return. The reason to structure your business in this way is to guard yourself from debtors or bankruptcy.

# Fictitious Business Name

In addition, if you decide to move forward as a Sole Proprietorship, you will need to register a Fictitious Business Name or DBA (Doing Business As) within the state you are conducting business. This is something you need to do only if you are using a business name different from your own legal name. For Example, if you are selling clothes under the label *"Trendy Designs,"* and your personal name is *Mary Smith*, you will need to file. This is also true if you are a corporation or LLC and you are selling a product under a different name from your corporation. So, if your corporation is *NIKOLAKI, Inc.* and you are selling clothing under the label *"NK Designs,"* you will need to file. Check with the state you live in as every state has slightly different criteria.

I KNOW!! This all sounds very complicated and might be much more information than you can understand or want at this moment in your career, but I offer up this advice just to help you understand what a serious undertaking it is to start your own business.

# Do Your Cost Sheet Honestly

When I met with the buyers at Henri Bendel, I had done a little bit of research beforehand, in the event that they would ask me prices. I found out that most of Henri Bendel's dresses sold in their Contemporary Dress Department for about $495 retail. To find out the wholesale price of a $495 garment, you normally have to divide it by a little more than half; the norm in the fashion industry for wholesale to retail is about 2.2 or 220%. In other words, a dress that retails for $495, wholesales for $225. This was the price I gave the Bendel buyers and naturally, they were happy about that as it sat perfectly in their sweet spot.

After we had finished celebrating and patting ourselves on the back for getting such a fantastic order; David and I sat down, calculator in hand, and did something we should have done *before* my meeting: We created a Cost Sheet. In our rush to have the dresses completed to show the buyers and our overall excitement with the opportunity to meet these influential people in the fashion industry, we somehow lost focus on the importance of properly costing our garments.

We quickly realized we had miscalculated the wholesale price of the dresses. After calculating the cost of the fabric, lining, notions (zipper, hang tape, etc.), pattern, grading, cutting, label, plastic bag, shipping + misc., each dress ended up costing about $400 WHOLESALE! Almost twice as much as I had told the buyers. Oops.

Not only that, but you might remember me mentioning that we created the dresses using a vintage polka dot print fabric. In order to manufacturer multiple styles of these dresses, we had to duplicate the fabric and have it custom printed! This brought the wholesale cost up even more. In other words, in our first ever order with a big department store, we were already going to lose money. And a lot of it. After beating ourselves up, we realized there was nothing we could do. There was no way I could somehow call the buyers in NYC and say "Remember when I said $225? I made a boo-boo, it was really $550." No way. We had only one option and that was to just suck it up and take a major loss. And learn a huge lesson in starting a business.

So, the obvious takeaway here is to always properly cost out your garments and be honest about what it will take to make money from your clothing. While it might be exciting and an ego-boost to be carried by a major department store, if you are not making any money, then you aren't really operating a business.

## How to Do a Proper Cost Sheet

So, what is a cost sheet and how do you properly cost a garment? A cost sheet is basically a report or chart that gathers all the costs for a garment. It helps you understand the monetary value of each item and assists you in determining a wholesale price for your clothing.

The essential components of a cost sheet should be:

- Material cost
- Trimming cost (buttons, zippers, hook & eyes, labels, etc.)
- Labor cost
- Packing material costs

In addition, a cost sheet should also include:

- Description of Garment
- Style #
- Season
- Size Range

And last but not least, a cost sheet should always include a front and back flat sketch. Often a fabric swatch of the material(s) is included.

After you do all your calculations on what it will cost to make one garment, double that price. This is how you get to make some money! For example: if you come up with $50 as the cost of materials and labor, etc., double that to $100, and that's the final wholesale price that you will sell to the store. The store will then take that $100 cost and multiply it by 2.2 to get the retail price which they will sell to their customer:

- $50 = raw cost x 100% = **$100**/Wholesale price
- $100/Wholesale price x 2.2 = **$220**/Retail price

This is a basic approach to costing garments for your business mainly if you are selling to boutiques or smaller stores. If you do get a larger order from a major department store or chain, then the calculations are different.

Because of the larger size of the order and the competitive pricing of department stores, the computations become a bit more complicated and severe.

*Did you know that a $149 dress at a store like Macy's or Nordstrom can cost the dress manufacturer just $22.35 to make?*

Let me explain . . .

Often times when selling garments to a large department store, you start from the retail price. Your sales rep will often tell the store your garment price has a 70% mark-up and that it retails for $149. What this basically means is that the raw cost of that garment is $22.35. You would then double that price to $44.70 for the wholesale cost. Now this is where it gets tricky . . . you then take 70% of that original retail price of $149 (which would be $104.30) and add it to your $44.70 wholesale cost making it a grand total of $149.

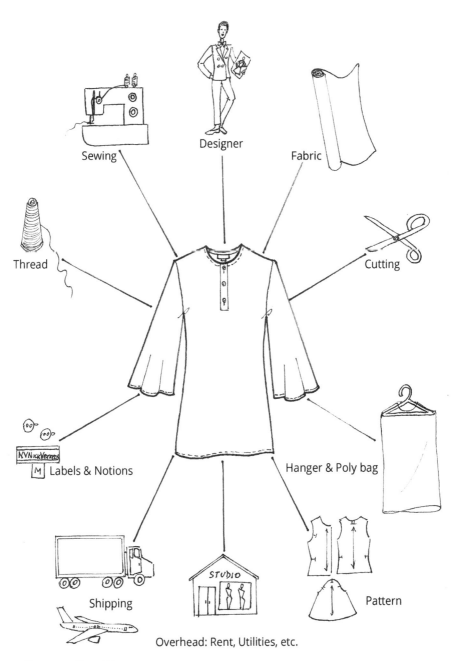

Sewing

Designer

Fabric

Thread

Cutting

Labels & Notions

Hanger & Poly bag

Shipping

Overhead: Rent, Utilities, etc.

Pattern

Garment Cost Diagram

## COST BREAKDOWN

$22.35 = **Raw Cost** (materials, trimmings, labor, etc.)
multiply by 2 = $44.70 **Wholesale Cost**

$149 x 70 = 10,430 divide by 100 = $104.30 (This is the **70% mark-up**)

Add $44.70 + 104.30 = $149 **Final Retail Cost of Garment**

| COST SHEET-- Woven Dress | | | | | |
|---|---|---|---|---|---|
| Date: | 7/25/2016 | | | Revised Date: | 8/27/2016 |
| Style #: | NK014SP16A | | | Season: | Spring 2017 |
| Size Range: | 2-14 | | | Market: | Contemporary |
| Label: | NIKOLAKI | | | | |
| Description: | Button Front Tie-Neck Dress | | | | |
| COMPONENT COSTS: | Yds./Qty | Unit Pr. | $ Amt | | Front Sketch |
| FABRIC: | | | | | |
| 100% Silk Twill/45" Wide | 2.0 | 11.50 | $22.00 | | |
| 100% Silk Habotai | 1.5 | 6.30 | $9.45 | | |
| Fusible Interfacing | 0.25 | 2.95 | $0.74 | | |
| | | | | | |
| | | | | | |
| TOTAL FABRIC COST: | | | $32.19 | | |
| | | | | | |
| TRIMS: | | | | | |
| Main Label | 1.0 | 0.06 | $0.06 | | |
| Size Label | 1.0 | 0.01 | $0.01 | | |
| Content/Origin/Wash Label | 1.0 | 0.08 | $0.08 | | |
| Buttons | 10.0 | 0.06 | $0.06 | | |
| Thread | 1.0 | 0.15 | $0.15 | | |
| Hangtag | 1.0 | 0.21 | $0.21 | | |
| | | | | | |
| TOTAL TRIM COST: | | | $0.57 | | |
| | | | | | |
| LABOR: | | | | | |
| Pattern | 1.0 | 2.50 | $2.50 | | |
| Grading | 1.0 | 1.50 | $1.50 | | |
| Cutting | 1.0 | 1.00 | $1.00 | | Back Sketch |
| Sewing | 1.0 | 35.00 | $35.00 | | |
| Wash | 1.0 | 1.25 | $1.25 | | |
| | | | | | |
| | | | | | |
| TOTAL LABOR COST: | | | $41.25 | | |
| | | | | | |
| PACKING MATERIALS: | | | | | |
| Hanger | 1.0 | 0.25 | $0.25 | | |
| Polybag | 1.0 | 0.05 | $0.05 | | |
| Shipping Box | 1.0 | 0.10 | $0.10 | | |
| Shipping Cost | 1.0 | 0.25 | $0.25 | | |
| | | | | | |
| | | | | | |
| TOTAL PACKING COST: | | | $0.65 | | |
| TOTAL COST: | | | $74.66 | | |
| WHOLESALE COST: | 100% | | $149.32 | | |
| RETAIL MARKUP | 70% | | $348.60 | | |
| RETAIL PRICE: | | | $498.00 | | |

Cost Sheet Final

Now this isn't just due to greedy department stores. Larger chain stores have high overhead costs that include employees, advertising and everything that is involved in running those huge stores. Also, it allows them the leeway to put a garment on sale multiple times, and still break even at 70% off their retail price. So basically, when you walk into a store and buy a dress for 50% off, the department store is still making some money.

What this all means to you is that you must do your cost sheets thoughtfully, meticulously and honestly. And don't forget to pay yourself! Even though I was making all the first patterns for our line (so we would save money on paying a patternmaker), we still had to figure out how to apply that cost into each wholesale price.

## From Mistakes to Positive Opportunities

Even though that first Henri Bendel order had unfortunate repercussions, it still opened many doors and gave us the impetus to continue and be a real fashion business. One of the realities of any business is making mistakes. Of course, the fewer you make the better off you are, but with mistakes come opportunities that can lead to benefits that will eventually add to the ongoing development of a fashion business. Making mistakes is part of maturing, not just as a person, but as a company.

Soon after our initial order with Henri Bendel, I finally got the courage to make appointments with various fashion showrooms that specialized in representing Contemporary clothing brands. Before that Bendel's order, I tried many times to make appointments with these showrooms but no one was interested since my clothing wasn't being carried in any stores. But now, those same showrooms were greeting me with open arms and double kisses. David and I eventually planted our line in a chic, upstart showroom at the California Mart in Downtown that was carrying the latest up-and-coming Los Angeles designers.

# Fashion Showrooms

If you aren't familiar with the way a Fashion Showroom works, let me explain. Showrooms are spaces where brands place their clothing lines to be represented. As the designer—or brand—you pay a monthly fee and commission of sales to have your clothing line displayed in a showroom space. So, instead of you trying to schlep your line to every store from here to Timbuktu . . . or asking a Macy's buyer to schlep over to your loft in that "Arsty" (read: seedy) part of town, you pay someone else to represent your line and sell it for you.

In the U.S. these wholesale fashion showrooms are usually located in New York or Los Angeles, the two "Fashion Capitals" of America; but they can also be found in major cities such as Dallas, Atlanta, Chicago and many more. Buyers from all over the country (and the world) come to the showroom during important Market Weeks or book appointments throughout the year when they are interested in seeing your new collection. They place the orders through the showroom and in turn, the sales representative then submits the order to you and your company. It then becomes your responsibility to produce and subsequently ship the order to the store once it's completed.

Once we secured our showroom, we began to expand our line. From that little humble beginning of just two dress styles, made for the Henri Bendel meeting, we expanded the collection to one that encompassed 20+ pieces, including jackets, pants, blouses and skirts. In the span of less than two years, we had received orders from Nordstrom as well as more than 100 stores across the U.S., Latin America and even Japan. NIKOLAKI was going worldwide. We were expanding and doing it at a rapid pace. We were excited to be getting orders, but also becoming concerned about the ability to fund our company and control the quality of our production.

# No Guessing Allowed

One problem with trying to expand your small business, is that while you need new orders to continue to survive, the more you take on, the harder it is to keep your business under control. We found ourselves in a bit of a Catch-22 situation. While we wanted to be carried in as many new stores as possible, the size of those orders were quite small and expensive to produce. This is often a problem for small clothing businesses and my advice is to stay focused and DO NOT speculate on the size and quantities you enter into production with. What does that mean? Let me explain:

When we started to receive a substantial amount of new orders, we instantly set out on a search for manufacturers to produce our clothing. We interviewed many small factories in Los Angeles that were happy to work with us, but wanted to cut and sew many more pieces than we needed. In other words, if we had an order for 20 dresses in one style, ranging in sizes from 2 to 12, these manufacturers were only willing to fabricate the garments if they could produce 100 dresses. This is called speculating (or guessing), in hopes that eventually you will be able to receive orders that match your inventory.

Luckily, this was not a mistake David and I made. Instead, I pulled out that trusty Rolodex I had acquired while working in the fashion industry and called up a few of the seamstresses I had worked with in the past. While it meant that I needed to drive all across Los Angeles picking up different garments from different sewers, it saved our business by not getting us stuck with a warehouse full of inventory. The common rule is to never produce more than 3% to 5% of your orders. As it is, you will undoubtedly get some rejected pieces and "bounced" orders from some of those fancy boutiques that were dying to carry your pieces.

# Don't Put All Your Eggs in One Basket

One of the benefits of having a showroom is that your clothing line will be seen by many more stores than if you were trying to make appointments with buyers yourself. We were lucky enough to have our collection "scouted" by the buyers at Nordstrom Department Store. After several appointments, follow up calls and emails, they placed an order. And not just any order . . . a substantial order that would be carried in stores across the country! Once again, the Champagne was flowing and we were ecstatic to be producing a significant amount of clothing and finally had the opportunity to use a larger manufacturer. We worked our tails off completing the order and jumping through all the hoops that a major department store requires in order to carry your clothing (more on that in the next book!).

We were thrilled to attend the launch of our collection at several of the stores including the Union Square Nordstrom in San Francisco. We loved chatting with the customers, seeing the women try on our garments and get valuable feedback.

What we soon learned about working with major department stores is that they require a high sell-through percentage. What this means is that they want your clothing to sell and sell FAST! Basically, they'd like you to sell anywhere from 35–50% of the inventory they ordered in 4 weeks. And if you don't? Well, let's just say there is a lot of wheeling and dealing going on behind the scenes. Either you take back the merchandise or give them what is called in the industry: markdown money. Yes, you heard me right, YOU pay THEM!

The lesson here is to not put all your eggs in one basket. If you gamble on the bigger stores and expect that they will stick with you and sustain your business, you could be in for a big surprise. My advice is to not allow one account to be more than 25% of your business. Keep your business varied and make sure you have customers across different parts of the industry.

## Risky Business

Getting your foot in the door in the fashion business is one of the toughest markets to crack. The lure of giving your clothing to stores on consignment might seem like a good idea at first, but trust me, you will most likely regret the decision. Consignment is basically lending your clothes in the hopes that it will eventually sell and you'll make some money. When you think about it, your designs are money spent. YOU paid for the fabric, YOU paid for the labor and YOU paid for your own time. Why would you be giving that away trusting that you will one day get something in return? The risk is too high and not worth the gamble. In addition, once the clothing hits the store racks, they become used. If it doesn't sell and is returned to you, it will most likely be slightly worn if not completely damaged.

# I'm Not Worthy

Every up-and-coming designer wants to be in the hottest boutiques. Not only is it a feather in your cap, but it also offers a bit of cachet for your brand and ammunition to be able to score some other key accounts. Unfortunately, those high profile stores aren't always the best bet for new companies. Do your research and find out how credit worthy those stores are. Often these boutiques are hot one day, and bankrupt the next. If the payment terms don't seem right, go with your gut and wait before taking them on as a customer. As hard as it might seem, it will save you in the end. I will never forget the excitement we had when we received orders from several of the TOP stores in the LA and San Francisco area, only for them to file bankruptcy a month after we shipped the merchandise. What did that mean for us? We lost the merchandise AND we didn't get paid! Sometimes these mistakes are unavoidable, but if you do a little research, you'll be surprised with the information you can find. Often those fancy stores look so nice because they've spent ALL their money on expensive fixtures!

# All Hands on Deck!

So there you are . . . you've applied some of my Tips & Tricks, you are getting some fantastic orders for you collection, and your business is growing! Fabulous, right? Yes, but with growth comes new obstacles and often times the bigger the business the bigger the problems. My advice is to not lose sight of your main goal. Don't let all the noise of a growing business fog your overall plan. While it is good to have a business plan and look forward to the next phase of your company, don't let that overtake the job at hand. Just because you have plotted out a sound business structure, do not be afraid to take a detour if that plan starts to fall apart. While you will obviously need help as your company grows, make sure that you are watching over and in control of all aspects of your line and especially production. If you don't have clothes that fit and don't reflect the high quality of your brand, you won't sell. In the end, the clothing business is all about the product, not good press. If your product doesn't fit well and you miss your shipping deadlines, your entire business could collapse literally overnight.

# Keep Focused

The world gives you signs. They arrive in all shapes and forms and can be both negative and positive. It is up to you to listen to them and not allow yourself to overlook "the writing on the wall" because you are afraid or overwhelmed.

When I received that fateful order from Henri Bendel for two simple dress styles, the Fashion Gods were sending me a signal that this was my path. I've always loved designing dresses, but as a young designer I felt compelled to "do it all." When I signed on with my Showroom, they enthusiastically encouraged me to do more. "More Tops! More Pants! More Jackets! Yes, Nick! You are amazing! You can do it all!" Well, it took me awhile before I realized that of course they want me to do more; the more product they have in the showroom, the more they can sell and make money! The only problem was, David and I were the ones doing all the work and spending all our money.

One of the most important pieces of advice I can give to designers is to STAY FOCUSED. Decide what you are good at or what people look to you to design and concentrate on that. Once you have become the "Designer Du Jour" of dresses, tops, t-shirts or whatever avenue you excel at, then you can begin to expand and grow your business. I'm constantly asked, "When are you going to do Menswear?" and my reply always is, "Let me be a success with Womenswear before I try to tackle another market." By focusing on your strengths, you will free yourself from the burden of becoming overwhelmed and ultimately allow yourself to excel at what you do best. You will also be happier, more fulfilled and undoubtedly your business will prosper.

# CHAPTER 8

# The Power and Pitfalls of Press

## Runway Realness

Right after our first order and subsequently getting our NIKOLAKI business in line, David and I were approached to join a Los Angeles organization called C.L.A.D., which stood for the Coalition of Los Angeles Designers. The coalition was made up of a select group of up-and-coming (as well as established and well-known) Southern California Fashion Designers. We would meet every now and then to discuss the trials and tribulations of running a fashion business, how to get funding, find sewers, fabric suppliers and exchange ideas to help each other out. It was really the first time I felt part of the "L.A. Fashion" community.

One of the highlights of being a member of C.L.A.D., especially during our first years in business, was having the chance to be part of L.A. Fashion Week and the C.L.A.D. Fashion Week Show. These shows quickly became the hottest ticket in town among all the fashionistas, and we were part of it, showing our collections! To this day, the shows we did through C.L.A.D. are some of my fondest memories of being a full-fledged (albeit up-and-coming) fashion designer.

If you have a chance to be a part of a local "fashion organization," especially one that involves designers supporting each other and putting on fashion shows, do it. This is something that can only help you grow as a designer and teach you valuable lessons about the industry. Frequently, you can feel isolated in the fashion business and too often you find it difficult to get assistance and knowledge from established designers. For whatever reason, whether it be their busy schedules, jealousy or fear of competition, good information can be hard to come by. Why not start your own Fashion Coalition and debunk the stereotype?! You'll be surprised how many young designers are in the same situation as you, with all of them looking to share their stories.

After being a part of C.L.A.D. for several years, David and I decided that we would make the leap and show our own runway presentation. The next Los Angeles Fashion Week was happening in a couple of months and naturally, we began getting the fashion show bug. We were in the process of finishing our next season's collection and decided it would be perfect timing for a grand debut.

We hired a fashion PR company to deal with all the logistics, including inviting the right clientele, organizing details and actually producing the event the night of the show. We also procured a fabulous space on the outskirts of Downtown Los Angeles near Chinatown, called the Woman's Building. The building, we found out, was the site of the very first Woman's Rights meeting in the early 1900s in Los Angeles. Therefore, we found it most appropriate to be celebrating women—through our fashions—on this prodigious site.

The inspiration for the show—and the collection—was "A Night in Marrakech." There were Moroccan, Middle Eastern and North African influences in some of the clothes including gold silk charmeuse harem pants, printed cotton voile tunics, and caftan-like silk gowns, so we took the exotic theme and ran with it! We used an Oriental rug as the runway, filled the venue with beautiful candles and even hired authentic Middle Eastern drummers to play during the show. It was a magical night.

We were thrilled to have a few celebrities in attendance, and got our first major press with *WWD, Los Angeles Times,* and *California Apparel News.*

Marrakesh Divas: NIKOLAKI Women's Building Fashion Show

Our "Woman's Building" Marrakech Diva Show was a big success and as a result, several months later we got word that Smashbox (the cosmetics giant) was mounting the first ever Smashbox L.A. Fashion Week at their studios in West L.A. They called us directly after hearing about our successful show and wanted NIKOLAKI to be one of the first designers to show.

Opportunities breed other opportunities and I'd like to think that the main reason we were selected was because our designs were fabulous and worthy of being on the Smashbox Fashion Week runway stage. But I also think it was because David and I were professional, we knew what we were doing, and we were easy to work with. We were humbled and honored to be there and took advantage of the opportunity in a positive way.

Mounting fashion shows can be very expensive. Major runway shows and venues can charge a fee of $50,000 to $150,000 for the location alone! Not to mention hiring the models, make-up artists, hair stylists, PR Company and more. Lots of (probably most!) fashion companies run successful businesses without ever showing in a single fashion week or doing one fashion show. But, at the same time, there are many Designer brands that use the Fashion Show format as part of their marketing strategy.

However, it is important to be honest with yourself as to why you are doing the fashion shows, especially if you are spending your own money. If the reason is for PR and marketing, fine. But if your goal is to get orders from those fashion shows, it rarely, if ever, happens. Be wary of people who say "You should do this fashion show because you never know . . . you might get orders . . . and there's going to be rich, important people in the audience who might be clients . . ." The fashion world is constantly changing and the reason for having a fashion show today is completely different from why they were mounted 30 or 40 years ago. In the beginning, the front row of a fashion show was filled with store buyers and high-end clientele. Now, the venues are filled with celebrities, magazine editors, industry press, and most importantly stylists and bloggers. In other words, it is a great way to generate press, but be truthful with yourself about whether or not your company has the funds to invest in such a risky proposition. While press is always important, store buyers usually bypass fashion shows and instead head straight to a showroom to see the clothes up close and personal.

We were lucky enough to be presented with opportunities that did not cost us large amounts of money. We had our venue costs waived and often bartered our clothing for certain models, make-up and hair. If these opportunities present themselves, then go for it! But don't get caught up in the hype and remember the real reason for your business: producing and selling beautiful clothing!

# K.Y.F.I.

Know Your Fashion Influencers. One of the most important things to do when getting your business off the ground is to educate yourself on who the fashion influencers are in your town and beyond. Whether it is the editor of *Vogue* or the style editor at your local newspaper, send them information on your line, website, press and invite them to an event or fashion show you are having. While you might not think that it is important enough to send to a prestigious editor or paper, you never know who will see it or if it will be something that might catch someone's eye.

I will never forget being invited to show my collection to the West Coast Editor of *Vogue* magazine. I had sent out endless packets about my collections and one day received an email to set up an appointment to meet with the esteemed Lisa Love. After picking myself up off the floor (and hoping it just wasn't a meeting to tell me to STOP bothering them!), I spent the next few days fine tuning my collection and making sure I had my presentation perfect. I even brought my dear model/friend Amara to make sure Lisa saw the clothing draped on a model. While nothing significant came from the meeting, it was an experience of a lifetime and something I learned from. When I look back at the experience, I know that I was a bit "green" for the prestigious pages of *Vogue,* but it gave me the education and a new level of understanding in what it takes to be considered for such a highly respected fashion publication.

Use this same tactic on fashion bloggers. I remember when we were first having our C.L.A.D. fashion shows, bloggers were just beginning to appear on the scene. Several of them wanted to attend our show but many of the designers brushed them off as being "cute fashion girls who just wanted to attend a party," so they sat them in the back. The "cute girl who wants to attend a party" might still be true, but they are now sitting front row and center. The fashion world has changed. Top style bloggers have millions of Instagram followers and get paid thousands of dollars to endorse products through social media. You may not have $100,000 to pay a fashion blogger to endorse your product, but at the very least, try and get their information and send them images of your designs, fashion illustrations, or an invitation to a show. You never know when they might show up, even if they aren't getting paid! You can at least try.

# Red Carpet Rundown

Boy how times have changed. Back in the day, the Red Carpet was literally something that was rolled out for people to walk over. Now, the "Red Carpet" has grown to become more than just something describing a floor covering, but an actual *industry*. It has evolved into the show before the show. From fashion magazines to celebrity "rags" all the way to prestigious newspapers and blogs, the Red Carpet is talked about throughout the entire world. Sometimes, the Red Carpet gets even more attention—and certainly more interest—than the actual event or awards show.

The annual Academy Awards Red Carpet has even been described as "The Biggest Fashion Show on Earth." Dressing celebrities and having them wear your designs has become big business and a very lucrative one, especially for the international fashion conglomerates. Everyone is dying to make their mark—and hopefully—make their money.

The Red Carpet has now gone beyond just Awards Season. This season used to be described as the months of the year when the Golden Globes, Screen Actors Guild Awards, Grammys and Academy Awards dominated the calendar. However, in recent times, it has become a year-round affair. The "Red Carpet" does not just describe the events before an awards show anymore; now the title can be applied to a movie premiere, a charity event, a party and even launching a product. Any occurrence where there might be press is now easily part of this "Red Carpet" umbrella.

On the Red Carpet: Nick Verreos at the Academy Awards

Not too long ago, I realized that something had changed when I began seeing actresses, showing up to a not-so-big movie premiere on a Tuesday night, wearing an $80,000 Elie Saab Haute Couture gown. That is the new normal when it comes to the Red Carpet world. While this recent phenomenon of Couture on a Tuesday has just started happening, the evolution of the Red Carpet has been steadily gaining strength with no slowdown in sight.

I realized early on that it was important for me, as a designer, to dress someone who was "famous" because I knew that it might add a bit of prestige to my resume and add cachet to my brand. I was also just happy that someone wanted to wear my designs, and if they happened to be beautiful and slightly well-known, then all the better. Loaning gowns to these people was a decision I consciously thought about with the promise that I would get a photo of them in my design, as well as return the dress in one, clean piece! But this isn't always the best strategy for every designer. It is a tricky business and you have to understand that there must be a benefit for both sides in order for it to be worthwhile.

Throughout my years in the industry, I've had my share of up's and down's regarding my designs on the Red Carpet. I've learned a lot in terms of how to maneuver this world. It is crucial to be diplomatic and wise and approach each collaboration with an end goal in mind. As much as actresses or singers love getting "free" clothing to wear on the Red Carpet, I, as the designer, need something in return. Whether it be a photo, promotion on social media or just the hope that the celeb says your name correctly when asked by the press, it is a manner of "Pay to Play" on both sides.

If you are looking to be a part of this world or are just interested in the behind-the-scenes inner workings, I'm going to give you a sneak peek into this crazy business. I'll end it with some "Nick Tips" and a helpful guide for young designers who want to get involved in dressing celebrities, as well as a bit of "Inside Dish" on what has become a very lucrative business.

## Who Have You Dressed?

Allow me to set this scenario: It had been about a year since David and I launched our line NIKOLAKI, and with my new found "fashion confidence," I set out with a plan to see if our line could be carried in local, Los Angeles-based stores. After doing my own research and scouting all the cool stores in L.A., I compiled a list of all the hippest, most-fashionable Contemporary boutiques. After finalizing the list I mailed the stores my "NIKOLAKI packages" with line sheets, photos and prices . . . the whole works. After a week, I followed up with phone calls to book appointments to show them the line.

Almost every single time I called, after I introduced myself and asked if they had received the package, the store buyer or manager would undoubtedly always ask "Who have you dressed?" and "Who has worn your designs?" I could not believe it. They wouldn't even ask me if I had been in other stores or how successful the line had been. Nope. All they wanted to know was if a celebrity, any celebrity—no matter how high or low on the alphabet—had worn my designs.

It bears repeating: I really couldn't believe it. But then, I thought for a second and realized where I was: L.A. I was just witnessing the beginnings of what would eventually become a "Who Have You Dressed" fashion industry.

## On the Red Carpet

My resume in having celebrities wear my designs really began many years before I even launched NIKOLAKI. Now, when I use the term "celebrities," I am extending the definition to include my beloved beauty pageant winners and contestants. In my pageant-loving world, these women were celebrities. In the early days, I had the wonderful opportunity to dress Miss Universe Sushmita Sen, Miss USA Ali Landry, and Miss Universe Brook Lee. For me, it was the perfect foray into the world of Red Carpet dressing. These were women I understood and fit perfectly within my "design wheelhouse." I made some fabulous gowns that brought my childhood dreams to life and in return, I started to get those coveted celebrity photos and had a few names to add to my resume.

From there, I started to gain the confidence to go after bigger names in the business. I am here to tell you that it is an industry of hits and misses. Early in my career, when I attempted to try to get celebrities to wear my designs, I received plenty of unanswered calls and emails, as well as some amazing propositions. However, the one thing I did learn is that you'll never know when the next opportunity might present itself.

Immediately following *Project Runway*, I was fortunate enough to get a bit of a "media boost" by being on the show. A PR agency called me to dress *Desperate Housewives* actress Brenda Strong for the SAG Awards. This was the first time I dressed someone for a major Awards Show and thankfully I received positive press in all the major magazines. Soon after that, I also had an absolute blast custom designing a gown for Kathy Griffin. She is every bit as funny off-screen as on! She was a delight to work with and looked gorgeous in my creation.

Carrie Underwood and her entire team are as sweet as you would expect. She wore one of our cocktail dresses on The Ellen DeGeneres Show and her appearance proved the power of television. The combination of a high-profile celebrity on a top rated TV show (wearing a beautiful dress!), can provide a huge boost to your business. The emails we received asking where to buy the dress Carrie was wearing were substantial and if you are lucky enough to direct those potential customers to a store or website, you are sure to make some money.

But sometimes the prestige and excitement of someone wearing your dress is the most thrilling payoff of all. One of the proudest moments in my career was when Academy Award-winning actress, Marlee Matlin wore my gown to the Oscars. It was the 80th Annual Academy Awards and we had received an email from a stylist who was working with the very talented Matlin, who had won the Best Actress Oscar for her performance in *Children of a Lesser God*. Matlin and her stylist decided on a black and white strapless silk satin gown with pleated bust detailing. After some major alterations (these actresses are TINY!), the day of the Academy Awards was approaching and we were pretty secure that Matlin would indeed be wearing our gown. But you still never know. Many times, you are told the actress will definitely wear your design, and you go ahead and call everyone and your cousin, from Los Angeles to Panama City and then (you know what I am going to say, right?), she never wears it. Trust me, I have been a victim of this very embarrassing scenario. I finally learned to keep my mouth shut until you see the actress on the Red Carpet with your very own eyes. This is most definitely a good lesson for any designer.

Luckily, Marlee did NOT have a change of heart and she looked absolutely stunning walking the Red Carpet. We finally sat back, hours later, watching the "Red Carpet Pre-Show"—with glasses of red wine in hand—happily content and relieved that we had accomplished a life-long dream of seeing one of our gowns at the Oscars.

Sketch of Marlee Matlin in NIKOLAKI

With the help of a fabulous PR Company and some wonderful stylists, we continued to dress some very high profile celebrities including Katy Perry, Beyoncé and the gorgeous Heidi Klum.

Sketch of Carrie Underwood in NIKOLAKI

Sketch of Heidi Klum in NIKOLAKI

Sketch of Katy Perry in NIKOLAKI

# Big Business

One of the very first questions I am asked about dressing celebrities on the Red Carpet is "Do the actresses actually pay for the dresses you design?" The answer is a resounding NO. I am continually shocked when I hear this question because I am surprised that everyone doesn't already know this. I am still asked by friends and family members if I made money from the dress that a certain celebrity wore. But I am here to tell you, once and for all, that this is not how the world of Red Carpet dressing works. Having celebrities wear your designs is a nice feather in a designer's "PR cap" and I learned early on the importance and prestige that went along with the Red Carpet; but press does not always translate to orders.

As a young designer, you have to decide whether this is a direction you want to take, and if indeed, you want to be part of this world. For anyone considering it, I have outlined some important topics that you need to know before diving into these often treacherous Red Carpet waters. Let's begin with the Business of the Red Carpet. . . .

The madness of dressing a celebrity has become much more difficult than it was back when I started working in the industry. It has become a multibillion dollar business. The rising importance of having a certain celeb wear your designs has also meant that bigger brands have entered into the mix and unfortunately young designers find it much more difficult to get their designs on a top level actress. That doesn't mean that it cannot happen, it just makes it that much harder.

It has been documented by many a fashion historian that perhaps the first designer who realized the importance of dressing celebrities for a big awards show was Giorgio Armani. He began his entry into Hollywood after dressing Richard Gere and Lauren Hutton in *American Gigolo*. But he secured his crown as King of the Red Carpet when at the 1990 Academy Awards, he dressed Michelle Pfeiffer in an elegant long sleeve navy gown, the same year Kim Basinger wore a One Sleeve White Satin Ball gown that was one step away from a costume. Now, over thirty years later, one can only describe what's occurred as a full-scale "invasion" of multinational fashion corporations taking over the Red Carpet world.

Dressing A-list celebrities for awards shows, movie premieres or even just to sit in the front row of a fashion show has become huge business, especially for the large fashion conglomerates. The major players in the industry include: LVMH/Louis Vuitton Moet Hennessy SE, who own Louis Vuitton, Dior, Givenchy, Marc Jacobs and Donna Karan. Kering, which is the parent company of Gucci, Saint Laurent, Balenciaga and Alexander McQueen; and Puig which controls Carolina Herrera, Paco Rabanne, and Jean Paul Gaultier. In fact, a handful of companies—principally six of them— dominate most of the fashion industry worldwide. And all these behemoths of style want a piece of the Red Carpet action.

# Money, Money, Money

During awards season, these fashion brands fly in top PR executives, designers, and teams of seamstresses from Paris, London and Milan, and put them up in luxury suites. This isn't to treat their employees to a lavish Beverly Hills vacation, but instead, these hotel suites become West Coast "ateliers" used as fitting rooms for all the actresses and nominees. If you spend the week before the Oscars on Rodeo Drive, you are sure to see more white vans with Fashion Logos like Chanel and Valentino, than you will see TMZ Tour Buses!

But this fashion frenzy doesn't just start the week prior to the awards; the business of Red Carpet dressing begins from the moment the nominees are announced. I have personally been in the presence of top Hollywood stylists on the day the nominees are announced. The moment the names are broadcast, the stylists are getting emails from all the PR executives, telling them that they are in town and would like to book appointments to show their new gowns. In other words, there is some serious pre-planning involved. These conglomerates know the game and have become serious players.

It has also become commonplace for an actress and her stylist to be paid for wearing a certain dress on the carpet. The payments are called "ambassadorships" and can be as high as $250,000 with a $30,000 to $50,000 fee going to the stylist. And let's not forget that the fashion house is spending about $100,000 to create these one-of-a-kind gowns, bringing the grand total close to $500,000! So what does this mean for new designers? Basically, they become important as back-up and brought in if deals (or dresses) fall apart. So, while the odds are becoming slimmer that a young designer will see their dress on an A-List actress at the Academy Awards, there are now endless events for you to make your mark and get a slice of that "Red Carpet Pie."

# Custom is the New Couture

Speaking of transformations—besides the revolution of the Red Carpet as a whole, the garments themselves have changed; not in terms of silhouettes but more about the *level* of gowns and designs. Back in the Golden Era of Hollywood, when actors were under contract to a studio, the executives would instruct the costume designers to create one-of-a-kind gowns for actresses attending the Oscars. However, as that era faded away and the ready-to-wear culture became the norm in the 70s and 80s, celebrities and nominees would simply just go shopping at Beverly Hills boutiques and department stores and actually buy (shocker!) their gowns. Some actresses would still have costume designers create one-of-a-kind designs for them (Hello Cher!), but this was becoming more infrequent. Slowly as designers like Armani began to influence the Red Carpet, stylists would pull gowns from high-end designer showrooms. These dresses were usually fresh off the runway and only from their Ready-to-Wear collections, or as they say in French, their *Pret-a-Porter*. While still quite pricey, (an average Ready-to-Wear gown can cost about $5,000-$15,000), they were not Haute Couture.

But then something changed. All of a sudden, nominated actresses or the latest "It Girl" started to appear on the Red Carpet wearing Haute Couture. In 2007, one would never see an actual Haute Couture gown at the Emmys or Golden Globes, but suddenly, a few years later, they became ubiquitous at award shows. In the past, these Haute Couture designs, which are all hand-made and cost upwards of $100,000 a piece, were deemed too delicate and untouchable, even for the Hollywood A-List crowd. Many fashion houses that had a Haute Couture arm in their brand portfolio, reserved these samples for actual clients that would order them. They were strictly off limits to anybody but the clients.

However, as the importance of the Red Carpet escalated and the fashion houses began to see the benefit of an actress in their gown, someone made the decision to release those prized gowns from their gilded Parisian closets and put them to work. In the past there was the fear that the Couture client might deem the sight of a Haute gown on the Red Carpet as being too bourgeoisie or déclassé. But it looks as if the rewards from Hollywood were too alluring for these brands to pass up.

It is rumored that there are only about 4,000 clients in the entire world who actually buy Couture, and the list is getting smaller and smaller as more women—even very wealthy ones—do not have a problem wearing Zara or even Top Shop. The fashion house executives realized that giving these one-of-a-kind, made-to-order creations more exposure would not hurt anyone, and in fact, it would be great marketing. Slowly but surely, one began to see more Chanel Haute Couture, Valentino Haute Couture, Giambattista Valli Haute Couture, Armani Prive, and Atelier Versace.

In the last few years, Red Carpet dressing has reached a new level, or some could argue has gone back to its origins. If you thought that Haute Couture was the pinnacle of dresses a celebrity would want to wear, think again. All of a sudden, "Custom" has come "en vogue". At first, it seemed to be a reaction from fashion designers who did not have Haute Couture or gowns in their collections to compete with the other brands. As a result, they asked themselves what the next best thing could be. The answer: Custom. Fashion houses like Prada, YSL and Gucci who all do not offer Haute Couture or gowns in most of their collections, suddenly started dressing A-List actresses in beautiful custom made gowns. These were one-of-a-kind dresses made especially for the Hollywood Glitterati and not available to anyone, even those 4,000 Couture ladies. Soon, all the top designers were luring celebrities to their label by sending them gorgeous custom illustrations meant exclusively for that oh-so-special actress. So, in a certain way, the Red Carpet has returned to its genesis, but now, with all new players and a lot more money involved.

## Publicity First

So by now, you might be asking yourself, what is the point for these fashion conglomerates to be spending millions of dollars lobbying actresses, their stylists and lending out $100,000 gowns? There are several reasons. The first is the obvious: Publicity. Having your brand's name mentioned and photographed on the Red Carpet and spread across the world via television and social media, is better publicity and often cheaper than running a national commercial during the Oscars telecast. In 2015, a 30 second commercial during the Academy Awards cost $1.95 million. Not only does that make loaning a dress seem like a bargain, but it can amount to more publicity with a broader reach, especially if the dress is a success. Photos of actresses in iconic gowns can circulate in the press for decades, and the brand and celebrity will forever be connected.

## Trickle Down Red Carpet Economics

Besides publicity, many people assume that the reason for fashion houses to dress celebrities is to sell more gowns. While some designers might see a slight bump in sales, this is mainly a myth. When a gown can cost upwards of $100,000 or at the very least $5,000, your consumer reach is incredibly limited. I don't need to tell you that women are not flocking to the stores to spend that kind of money on clothing, let alone a dress for a special occasion.

But now, if I told you that it was only $40, and you could go to the store or purchase it online immediately, then I'm sure your response would be completely different. This is what happened the year Sharon Stone arrived at the Academy Awards in a black gown-skirt and a Gap t-shirt. The next day, everyone and their mother wanted that t-shirt and sales went through the roof. Why? Because it was accessible and cheap.

Contrary to what some people might think, "Martha from Missouri" will not see the gown Jennifer Lawrence wears on the Red Carpet, for example, and then head to the Dior boutique on Rodeo Drive and order one for herself. The real reason is because they want our imaginary "Martha" to hear "Chanel" or "Dior" over and over again, in the hope that she might end up at her local department store, see a bottle of Chanel perfume, or Dior makeup, and say to herself "Oh, wasn't Jennifer Lawrence wearing Dior at the Oscars? I think I'll buy this Dior lipstick!" It is as simple as that. It's what I like to call "Trickle Down Red Carpet Economics".

The big fashion brands know that most of the viewing public cannot afford a $100,000 Haute Couture gown, but they sure can buy a $35 lipstick, a $75 bottle of perfume, $200 sunglasses or even splurge on a $4,000 Chanel handbag. This is the real reason why those fashion companies dress the celebrities. It is not by accident that all of these brands have makeup, perfume and skincare lines; not to mention their accessories, which are much more accessible to 99% of the population. On top of all that, it also becomes an incentive for a young actress to choose a certain multi-million–dollar fashion conglomerate. There is always the chance that the beautiful celeb will generate enough press, so the brand will hire her as a spokesperson. So, not only has this become big business for the fashion companies, but also for the celebrities as well.

# Nick Tips

Even though the Red Carpet fashion landscape is becoming increasingly treacherous and difficult for a small up-and-coming designer, there is one light at the end of this tunnel: Red Carpet events continue to be very popular and there are seemingly limitless opportunities to dress celebrities. The Golden Globes, SAG Awards, Emmys, and Academy Awards are not the only "Red Carpet" games in town. Every single week, whether in Los Angeles, NYC or beyond, there is an event in which a celebrity needs to look fabulous. These are the opportunities for the young designers to make their mark and gain some publicity. Below are a few tips that I think will help you plot a course and survive in the competitive world of the Red Carpet.

## Be Selective

When you decide that indeed you want to have people wear your designs for Red Carpet events, be weary of saying "Yes" to dressing everyone. I know this may sound harsh but it doesn't benefit you to lend a free gown to the wife of a movie producer (for example) who will never, ever be photographed by the photo wire services. The whole point of you—as a designer—lending your clothing for free, is to get a photo and make sure that person is at the very least, slightly or remotely "famous." Trust me, lending your gown for free to that producer's wife is not going to benefit you in any way. Unless, she is famous herself. Once word gets out that you will lend your dress to anybody, stylists might take advantage of you. Before you know it, your gown was worn to an event, never even photographed and all you are left with is a dirty dress with makeup stains! So, while it is important to get your clothing out there, it is also crucial to be cautious and selective.

## Get to Know Stylists

From the moment I began working in the fashion industry, I would network, network, network. I would attend fashion events, parties and even nightclubs in order to connect with people that might be interested in working with me. I call it "Fashion Schmoozing." Because I lived in Los Angeles, you could be having brunch at some random restaurant and inevitably bump into someone who said that they were a Stylist. So, I realize it might be easier in L.A., but the same could probably be said about NYC and other major cities like Miami, Chicago or Atlanta. Wherever you might be located, always keep your eyes and ears open for making a connection with like-minded people who can help you achieve your fashion goals and don't leave your house without a business card.

Another way I got to know stylists early in my career was by literally researching celebrities and who dressed them. If you search the internet, there are actual lists of stylists and the celebrities they dress. But, you can also dig deeper and research through Instagram, Twitter, and other social media platforms. Make sure to follow all the stylists you admire and stay up-to-date on their current client roster. Compile a "wish list" of the stylists and celebrities that you want to work with and while it is fine to dream big, also try to be realistic about your goals. Understand that you might not be able to connect with the top people in the industry right away. Make sure you have some artists on your list that are more attainable. Mail them a Look Book of your designs, and email them photos or a link to your website. And always follow up!

## Be Your Own PR Director

Promote, promote, promote! If you cannot afford to pay a PR agent to promote your line, then you have one choice: Do it yourself! Photograph your line, whether it is on models, dress forms or mannequins and show them off on your Social Media accounts. You never know when a stylist might come across one of your postings, like what they see, and get in touch with you to borrow one of your designs for a celebrity client. And if you are really lucky, you might get an actual up-and-coming actress, who sees your designs on Instagram and wants to wear it! Always stay open to collaborations, as you never know where a connection might lead.

## Pay to Play: Showrooms

The premiere way to get publicity for your clothing and almost guarantee that you will have your line worn by celebrities, is to enlist the help of a public relations showroom. There are several top fashion showrooms that are exclusively in business to provide clothing to stylists to then be worn by their celebrity clientele. Most of these "Red Carpet" Showrooms are located in either Los Angeles or NYC and ironically, can be difficult to locate since they themselves don't always have the best websites. (Let's hope it is because they are devoting so much time and energy to their clients!) One effective way of finding out the names of these showrooms is by looking up other fashion designer's websites and clicking on their "Contact" page. Many designers will have the name, address and contact phone number of the PR showroom that represents them.

Also, there are different types of these PR fashion showrooms. If you decide to work with a showroom to get your designs on celebrities, do yourself a service and find out what other lines they carry and make sure your collection is comparable. If your clothing line is more evening, you should be in an evening-centric fashion PR showroom. If your line is more sportswear, you should search out a representative that reflects your style.

There are pros and cons to being in these showrooms. Let me start with the con: It costs a lot of money. Be ready to shell out thousands of dollars a month to have your line represented. The decision to spend that amount of money on press needs to be considered very sensibly and it needs to be part of your overall business plan. If it works within your budget and you see the benefit being reflected in sales, then it is an important component to becoming successful. But, if you spend every last cent on generating press and have no money left for production or see no increase in revenue, then it is nothing more than a self-indulgent pat on the back.

The pros are several. First, these PR showrooms are very well known in the industry and many stylists visit them on a weekly basis for their clients. It's a one stop shop for them and as an up-and-coming designer, you could never have the depth of contacts that these PR agencies can provide. Also, these showrooms take the burden away from you having to personally meet with every stylist and assist them in checking in and out your garments. Trust me when I tell you that the task of being your own personal PR person can be incredibly time consuming. In addition, a nice incentive in having a PR representative is that someone else can play the job of Good Cop/Bad Cop. It is incredibly helpful to have someone besides yourself weed out the good clients and the bad clients. You won't have to feel awful about rejecting that Producer's wife or tracking down lost and damaged garments. Outsourcing your public relations helps you streamline your job and allows you to focus on the job at hand: Designing.

## The Gift of Giving

Dressing celebrities, by the way, is not exclusive to evening wear designers. Many a t-shirt company has a "celebrity" page on their site. One way for sportswear and activewear brands to get that much needed hit of publicity, is by participating in a Gifting Suite. Gifting Suites and Lounges are locations where companies give products to celebrities in exchange for photos being taken of them wearing or holding your product. These usually occur the days prior to awards shows and are ubiquitous in Los Angeles before every major event. As a brand or designer, you pay these companies a fee (from hundreds to thousands of dollars) to set up a booth or section at the location where the Gifting Lounge will be held. It is the responsibility of the event producer to invite the celebrity clientele. By "gifting" the celebrities your product, you kindly ask for them to pose with your clothing, jewelry or whatever your product might be, and secure a photo which then can be promoted. These gifting suites provide varying degrees of success, mainly dependent on the level of celebrity the event organizers are able to provide. Obviously, the gifting suites that have access to a higher level of clientele are more costly. For example, during the lead-up to the Golden Globes or Academy Awards, if you are able to get a high profile nominee to attend, you will surely be paying a premium. Although it must be noted that true A-List celebrities would most likely never attend an "open" event. A movie star that makes millions of dollars would not find the need to trade their notoriety for a few free items and they are probably contractually obligated to specific products anyway. In addition, these gifting suites work better for the designer or company if their product is low in cost. If you are able to manufacture t-shirts or sandals that have a low wholesale price, you will definitely get more "bang for your buck."

## Is Dressing a Celeb for You?

Dressing celebrities has increasingly become an important arm of any designer or brand's marketing portfolio. I have told you why a fashion conglomerate wants their dresses on the Red Carpet, but what is the reason for a young designer? While you might not have a perfume or cosmetics line, the goal is to build your business so that one day you might! Dressing celebrities is a way of getting your name—and your line—out there. The old adage of "you have to shout to be heard" can be used in fashion by dressing a celebrity in your designs and hoping they will literally "shout" your name to a TV camera. It can be an incredibly useful tool in promoting your company, but you need to have a strategy and make sure that it does not overwhelm your business. It is important to be judicious with both your time and your dollars. Understand that this is just a small portion of your business and not the entire reason for you being a designer. It's wonderful to have your clothing worn by celebrities on the Red Carpet, but if that is the entire component of your company, then you definitely will not survive. You have to realize that dressing actresses is a marketing strategy that is just a small slice of your "designer pie."

# CHAPTER 9

# Project Runway: Dish from the Runway, Workroom, and Beyond

## You're In!

When you go to a *Project Runway* audition, there are only three outcomes that they tell you: "Yes," "Maybe," and "No." I will never forget, after I introduced myself and presented the lovely model Amara in my gown, Tim Gunn turned to me and said "Well Nick, we love you and . . . You're In!"

Getting a "Yes" from the audition judges doesn't instantly mean that you are on the show. It basically just signifies that you made that very important "first cut." The producers then told me that I was to make a video of myself, showing my design environment and essentially give them a sneak peak of who I was as a designer. I remember having to borrow a friend's camera to do my short video and enlist her help in directing and editing. I will also never forget almost missing the deadline. It was due on a certain day of the week at 5 p.m. at the Downtown Los Angeles office of the production company Magical Elves, and I got there at 4:59. Typical. I am on "Venezuelan" time.

A week or so after I turned in the video, I received a call saying that I made the second cut. Hooray! From that point, there were only two further procedures in getting the final "You're really in!": the requisite background check and a psychological test. Somehow I passed both: Hooray again and thank goodness! One or two weeks later I received a phone call, and it was from Tim Gunn, officially telling me that indeed, I was on Season 2 of *Project Runway* . . . and I was to receive a secret box in the mail with my first challenge. Oh yeah, and I was to leave for New York to begin shooting in one week!

# The First Challenge

When I found out that I was going to be on *Project Runway*, I was excited, nervous and most of all, in a state of panic. Being on the show would require that I leave my daily life of designing and teaching for about a month. Some people don't realize this, but you basically shoot a new episode and embark on a new challenge every couple of days. In other words, if you last the whole season it is about twelve challenges in 4 weeks!

I knew that the daily grind of running NIKOLAKI would be safe in David's hands, but it was the teaching part that had my stomach tied up in knots. How was I to leave my students in the middle of their assignments, find substitutes for all those classes and let them finish the quarter without me, with little to no explanation? Part of being on a reality competition show is that you cannot tell anyone what it is that you are doing and why you have to be gone. But naturally, I had to tell the college and more specifically, my department directors. I explained that the show was about fashion designers competing in design challenges and that I would do my best to make them— and FIDM as a whole—proud . . . and I added that they couldn't tell anyone!

Finally, everything was set for me to leave for filming in New York City. I was feeling more confident and less stressed about my imminent departure when suddenly my doorbell rang and a box arrived on my doorstep. There were instructions to open it alone,

Project Runway Season 2 First Challenge: Nick Verreos Design

without anyone else around. It was very *Mission Impossible*. I did as I was instructed. As I opened the box, there was another note that I had to read before inspecting the rest of the contents. The note read as follows: "Congratulations for making it onto Season 2 of *Project Runway* . . . This is your First Challenge!" I was to design and create a garment that best showed who I was as a designer and bring the completed garment with me to New York. The box contained six yards of muslin and $20 to spend for trims, zippers and notions. I decided to create a gown (of course) as well as an accompanying jacket. I also dyed the dress to add interest to an otherwise bland muslin fabrication. My final creation turned out to be quite nice and I must say, very representative of my design aesthetic.

Something rather amusing yet seemingly quite dramatic happened to me on my trip to purchase notions. Once I had settled on my design and was ready to start my work, I went Downtown to the largest fabric store in LA to buy thread, zippers and notions. I had been inside the fabric store all but two minutes when I overheard a woman who was on her phone speaking loud enough for me to hear her across the store. She was asking questions such as, "Can I purchase tools with this $20?", "Is tax included in the total amount spent?", and "Do we need to use the entire amount of money?" I knew instantly that she must be another contestant on the show and because of the fear the producers had already instilled in me, I literally hid behind a bin of fabric and then ran out of the store! I waited in the parking lot for half an hour until I felt like it was safe to re-enter. Looking back, I have no idea what I was so afraid of, but at the time it was a do-or-die moment.

It turns out that the woman in the store was indeed to be a contestant on my season of *Project Runway*. Her name was Kirsten Ehrig and before becoming a designer, she originally studied law; hence all the detailed questions!

# The Flight I Missed, the Friend I Made

The day I was to depart to NYC for *Project Runway*, I put on my most FAB and fashionable outfit and headed out to LAX with David as my trusty driver. Naturally because of typical Los Angeles traffic and my aforementioned "Venezuelan Timing," we were late. Very late. David and I said our tearful "Goodbyes," I ran to the gate and lo and behold, I missed my flight.

My stomach dropped as I thought, right then and there, that my chances to be America's Next Top Fashion Designer, were *finito*. Done. I tried to reach in my bag to find the emergency phone number of a production assistant to tell them the news and to apologize profusely. Suddenly a stylish young guy approached me, seeing me sweating— in my Dior sunglasses—and talking loudly on the phone (I guess my Kirsten Ehrig experience had rubbed off on me). He then quietly turned to me and said "Are you going to New York for a 'secret' show?" "YES!" I replied, "Are you too?" Indeed he was, and he also had missed the flight. Oh thank goodness I was not alone. From that moment John Wade became my best friend.

We eventually made it on the next flight to NYC and we were only slightly off schedule. Once we got our seats on the plane we never said another word to each other until the first day of filming. It was our little secret. I think we were so scared of the producers and their "Don't talk to anyone!" rules that we wanted to abide by them in case they had spies on the plane. John, unfortunately, became one of the first casualties of our season when he and one of the other designers, were the first contestants to get the *"Auf Wiedersehen"* from Heidi Klum. However, something wonderful did result from our fateful LAX encounter and from being on the show together—albeit for him short and sweet: To this day, over ten years later, I consider John one of my best friends for life.

## What are Pattern Blocks?

Before leaving for *Project Runway*, the producers sent information on what we could and could not bring with us. We were told in very general terms to bring our "tools and supplies" that would pertain to construction only. In fact, an actual "tool kit" was never mentioned, but most designers would realize that this would be part of the overall kit. I called the producers and asked them if it was permissible to also bring my pattern blocks. These are not actual garment patterns but are foundation patterns made from manila paper that aid in creating other garments. In essence, if I was to make a certain skirt design, I can use my "Basic 2 dart Skirt" block to help me in designing another more complicated skirt.

Needless to say, the producers had no idea what Pattern Blocks were. Their area of expertise is filming so if you asked them about casting, lighting or cameras, they'll know a lot; fashion pattern blocks, not so much. I never got an answer so I brought my blocks. From watching Season 1 of *Project Runway*, I knew that we would be under severe time constraints (that's the point of the show!) and using my pattern blocks might, at the very least, aid me in cutting the time I spent in pre-draping/patterning.

Once I arrived in NYC for the show, we did not begin officially filming until a couple of days later. All the designers were sequestered and during that time, I asked the producers once again if it was OK to bring my blocks. I didn't want to be in trouble for having an unauthorized design aid and I especially did not want that scene caught on camera to make me look like a fool.

It was literally the first day of filming and we were in front of Parsons about to meet Heidi Klum and Tim Gunn for the very first time, and I asked a third time about my pattern blocks. One of the executive producers said "Let me see if we can ask Tim, since he would be the person with the most knowledge on the subject." Soon enough, I received word that in fact, I could NOT bring my pattern blocks. So, sadly they remained at the bottom of my suitcase where, for the next four weeks, they never saw the light of day. I always am glad I was honest and upfront with the producers, especially after seeing the fate of poor Keith Michael in Season 3, who brought pattern books with him for some "night-time reading." Interestingly enough, we were never told NOT to bring pattern books. I guess, like my blocks, they were considered to be too much of a fashion advantage.

# Fashionably Anonymous

Let's go back to 2005. That is the year Season 2 of *Project Runway* was filmed. The show had only debuted six months earlier on a cable network which until then, was known for *Queer Eye For The Straight Guy* and showing reruns of *The West Wing*. Not many people watched the first season of *Project Runway*, and in fact, according to Bravo's former President Lauren Zalaznick, the ratings were initially dismal.

Essentially, no one cared or gave a second look at the sight of a dozen or so stylishly dressed people walking around the streets of Manhattan with Tim Gunn in tow. No one really knew who Tim Gunn was for that matter, and seeing fashionable 20- and 30-somethings in Manhattan... that's called an average Tuesday in NYC.

One of the fondest memories from my time on *Project Runway* was the fun anonymity of it all. I remember walking out of Parsons with all my fellow designers on one of our many trips to Mood, the fabric store featured on the show. We would walk right out of the front door of the college and all together—like a group of school kids going to a museum—stroll through the streets of NYC without anyone even giving us a second look. I remember laughing about it as we wondered "what do these NYC tourists think?" Every now and then, because we always had several camera people in tow, we would get asked by someone if we were filming a show. Of course, we would never give them a true answer, but even if we did, I'm sure 99% of the people would still be perplexed and then ask "What's *Project Runway?*"

I venture to guess that things have changed significantly for current designers on the show. I am sure that a lazy stroll down the streets of Manhattan is unheard of now and certainly walking in a group with Tim Gunn would be out of the question. I've heard stories from former contestants about vans with blackout windows and decoy contestants to throw off any fans that might catch a glimpse of the designers outside of their workrooms. I'm not surprised that things have changed; the Emmy-nominated show has been a huge hit for years now and a TV phenomenon. But, I feel honored and lucky to have had those anonymous walks to Mood, with a dozen or so designers, Tim Gunn and three camera people following us. Those are special memories that I will never forget.

## Fashion Comrades

Even though filming *Project Runway* is very stressful and it is a competition that pits designers against other designers, there is bonding and sometimes long-term friendships that evolve; at least that was my experience. While I don't get to speak with most of my fellow Season 2 alum very often, I will always feel connected to the cast and whenever I do unite with any of them, we are always able to pick up right where we left off. There is definitely a bond that connects us as I truly feel we were comrades in a "fashion battle."

## John Wade

I spoke of my immediate bond with John Wade back when we were supposed to depart on our all-important flight to NYC. Like I said before, he was voted out in the first challenge but even in such a short time, I knew immediately that he was "Good People." Days after he was voted off, we paused from filming to shoot the promos and ads for the show. We were all transported to the Silvercup Studios in New Jersey (where they filmed *Sex And the City*) and had a rare break from the competition and had a fun day doing photoshoots and promotional videos. John was amazing. You would have thought that he might be bitter or slightly resentful from being eliminated from the show and still having to participate in the day's activities. However, he couldn't have been more delightful and genuinely happy to be there; always smiling and overtly wonderful to everyone. I'm sure he was relieved to not have the stress of the show, but it must have been hard not to be disappointed. He taught me a lesson by his behavior: Smile and be nice, it goes a long way.

## Raymundo Baltazar

I also bonded with Raymundo Baltazar. He was one of the younger contestants, but he was an old soul when it came to his knowledge of fashion, fashion designers and fashion history. Speaking to him was like talking to your kooky aunt who has "lived the life." I immediately took a liking to him and his "old soul" personality. We also bonded over the fact that we were both Latino and we would talk to each other in Spanish all the time. We chatted about our designs, what we were doing and yes, gossiped about some of the other designers while the cameras were rolling. Understandingly this annoyed the producers to no end. We were constantly being reprimanded for speaking Spanish since they couldn't use any of this on the show and their budget didn't include subtitles. We just laughed and thought "Well, if this ever gets shown in Latin America, we'd be a hit!" I am still good friends with the fabulous Raymundo and we still chat in Spanish when we want to talk about other people!

## The Boys of 35D

My roommates on the show were Andrae Gonzalo, Daniel Vosovic and Santino Rice. We were all in one apartment, 35D to be exact, at the Atlas Apartment Building. The living quarters were quite spare and the whole environment had a dormitory feeling to it. Honestly, I was just happy to have a bed and be able to rest my weary head after the very long and stressful filming days. Many people don't realize, but we were usually up by 6am and the cameras didn't leave our apartment until midnight.

The producers did try and stock our refrigerators with liquor, but we rarely ever took advantage of it. By the time we would get back to the apartment after working on a challenge, it would be past midnight, and we would be beyond exhausted and too tired to even break open a beer or make a cocktail. I'm sure the producers would have loved us if we did, so they could capture an ensuing drinking party on camera but alas, it never happened.

Andrae, Daniel, Santino and I all got along from the start. I enjoyed Andrae for his easy-going personality and I also bonded with him because he was from L.A. Daniel was a dynamic individual and someone who had that "it" factor. He had only graduated from FIT one month before filming, so he was definitely a "fashion baby," but his talent was undeniable and he also had that same old soul character that Raymundo possessed. During one of the challenges when I was ready to give up, Daniel was the one that brought me back to reality and made me remember the reason I was on the show. Even though he was 15 years younger than me, in that instance, he became the adult in the room.

Coincidentally, I knew Santino from Los Angeles as well. The night prior to the first day of filming I ran into Santino in the hallway of the hotel (clearly, back in the early seasons, the producers didn't

Boys of 35D

have the sequester program very well organized!). After the initial shock of seeing each other, we exchanged knowing looks as to why we were both there, and Santino exclaimed "we are both going to kick some a\*\*!" Because Santino and I knew one another and admired each other's talent, we both seemed to silently have a strategy to team up and pool our talent in order to advance. Unfortunately, as was apparent in the Lingerie and Banana Republic challenges, the fact that we were both talented did not equate to making a strong team.

With that being said, Santino's bigger than life personality could be a ton of fun. We amused ourselves with the song "Daniel Franco where did you go?" as well as Santino's infamous impression of Tim asking "Where's Andrae?" in that droll Tim Gunn voice. Only Santino could get away with that. Everyone asks how that all came about and it was really because Andrae would somehow always be in the sewing room when Tim wanted to do his "Tim Visits." Naturally, Tim asked "Where's Andrae?" and by the fifth time he asked, well, it just became fodder for becoming THE tagline of our season. Tim was nonplussed, to say the least, but he was always a good sport.

Strike a Pose:
Kara Janx and Nick
Verreos on the way
to Mood

## Chloe, Kara, and Emmett

I had lots of fun with some of the ladies in my season, especially Kara Janx and Chloe Dao. I liked them both for the same reason: they were sassy gay men trapped in women's bodies! During the stressful workroom time as well as on our walks to Mood, Kara would be a fun, lively respite from the madness. I was slightly surprised when I watched the show to see the very stressed out version of Kara. While I experienced the "cut and cry" drama in action, I had many more light-hearted moments with her than dramatic times. Chloe was almost like a "Mom" figure, always putting things correctly in perspective, and not holding back from telling it "like it is" if anyone asked for her opinion. She was a hard worker, fearless and most of all talented, which was proven by her winning the show!

Chloe Dao, Nick Verreos, and Emmett McCarthy at EMc2

I also have to single out Emmett McCarthy. Emmett was quiet and unassuming and I think I bonded with him because we were closer in age. But it wasn't until he was eliminated that I really appreciated him. At some point during the course of filming I mentioned to Emmett that I wished I had kept a diary, since things were moving so fast and I'd probably never remember half of what we were experiencing. After Emmett's elimination, I received a diary from him with a timeline documenting every challenge with descriptions and dates. Emmett did not have to do that and it was such a classy and thoughtful gesture, which to this day, I much appreciated. Emmett then went on to open a fabulous boutique in NY and he generously invited fellow *Project Runway* alum to sell their clothing in his store. We had fantastic events that helped unite *Project Runway* fans and the designers they admired. He has been such a generous supporter of his fellow designers and the show.

# Model Walk-Off

One of the most controversial things that happened during my season was the infamous Zulema "Model Walk-Off." We were well past the halfway point of the season and heading into the eighth challenge. Prior to this episode, and in all the previous challenges, every winning designer stuck with their original model. When the episode began and Heidi asked the winner if they wanted to change their model, no one ever did. So by this time, we had grown very fond of our own models and I especially took a liking to the gorgeous Tarah Rogers. As a fashion designer, I tend to have a special affinity toward my models, as I often look to them for inspiration and they make my designs come to life. I was incredibly excited from the very first challenge to get Tarah; she was beautiful, had the perfect figure, was tall, and walked like a runway diva!

Besides all this, sticking with the same model benefits you in the competition as you learn to work with your models proportions. In my season, no one wanted to switch their model, except for one person: Zulema. Zulema Griffin was the designer in our season who loved to stir the pot. Early on, she had a fit about her model form and threw a tirade about her muslin being missing. The camera people followed her every move and complaint and were always ready and waiting for what she might do next. She had won the previous challenge which involved designing a costume for Olympic figure skater Sasha Cohen, but throughout the challenge, you could tell that Zulema and her model were not getting along.

The time came for Heidi to ask her infamous "Do you want to stay with your model?" question and since Zulema had won the challenge, it was her time to answer. No one was expecting her to change her model but I had a sneaking suspicion that she might.

Here's why: I had noticed that right before the scene was filmed and we were being called out of the workroom, the camera, sound and production staff were all barely making eye contact with me and when they did, they had a "poor him" look on their face. I didn't really pay any attention to this until Zulema told Heidi that she DID indeed want to change her model. Not only that, but she upped the drama quotient and declared that in order to decide which model she would pick, she wanted to make three models have a "Model Walk-Off." The minute she did that, my heart just sank; I knew that she would pick Tarah. And she did. At the time, I was both angry and sad. It didn't help that all my fellow designers kept saying "Oh My God, I can't believe she just did that!" Of course, it was in the rules and Heidi did ask each winner in every episode if they wanted to change, so we all knew it was a possibility, but it still was a shocker to all of us. I certainly do not condemn her for doing it now, and think it was a pretty strategic game play, however at the time, I was devastated.

## My Favorite Challenges

I'm sure it comes to nobody's surprise that the "All Dolled Up" challenge was my favorite; after all, I won it! The challenge was to create a look for Mattel's "My Scene Barbie." Since she was considered the cool, younger version of Barbie, I wanted to design a fun, sassy, Miami Beach-meets-Mykonos look. I found a fantastic abstract print at Mood and paired it with a bright green jersey. I was so inspired and finished so early that I decided to add a matching printed head turban, since why not? I looked around at the other designs in the workroom and secretly knew I had this one in the bag. Although, I still remained quite reluctant to start doing a winning happy dance since you never know, especially with *Project Runway*.

I was so happy for the win. Especially because all I could think about was my young niece, who was all but 5 years old at the time, playing with her very own "Uncle Nick" Barbie. This would hopefully make me the best—and coolest—uncle ever!

My second favorite challenge was titled "On Thin Ice," and involved designing a figure skating costume for Olympic silver medalist Sasha Cohen. My partner David has been a life-long fan of figure skating. He

Uncle Nick with his niece Casia dressed as his Project Runway Barbie

analyzes the scores and knows all the technical details. So, while I also considered myself a fan, in the beginning I was more like a "football wife," before really getting involved in the sport.

Project Runway Barbie: Nick's Winning Design

On Thin Ice: Nick Verreos's Design for Olympic figure skater Sasha Cohen

Filming of this episode began quite interestingly and colorfully. We found boxes of bright Lycra leotards (and accompanying stretchy black pants for the boys) in our apartments. We were then transported via vans to New Jersey. We had absolutely no idea what we were doing there, until the van pulled into the skating rink and I started shaking with excitement. We all walked in, put on our ice skates and were told to get on the ice. Suddenly, Olympic figure skater Sasha Cohen appeared and that's when I lost it!

The cameras captured me jumping up and down like a teenage girl who was just about to meet Justin Bieber. I began pushing my fellow designers saying "Oh my God!! It's Sasha Cohen!!! OMG!!!" They had no idea who she was and more specifically, why I was acting as if she was Beyoncé! Well, because to me, she was like Beyoncé! I was a big fan of Cohen and her figure skating career, so imagine all of a sudden, getting the chance to design a figure skating costume for her. I loved it! The entire time I was working on the design, I kept thinking "Wait until David watches this episode! He'll DIE!" I didn't win and wasn't one of the top favorites, but I didn't care. I was just so happy to have had the chance to design and create a figure skating ensemble for Sasha Cohen on *Project Runway*. I kept this challenge a secret and did not tell David about it, until the episode aired seven months later. You can only imagine the Viewing Party madness we had that night in our home watching that episode.

## My Not-So Favorite Challenges

I would be remiss if I did not say that the challenge in which I was eliminated was my No. 1 Not-So Favorite Challenge, for the obvious reason. The episode was titled "Makeover" and was the tenth challenge, right before deciding who the Top Four finalists would be. We were to create an outfit for one of our fellow designers. I designed and created a suit for Daniel Vosovic. I actually liked what I made and designed for him. I wanted to do a skinny suit and make him more European and elegant looking. I was actually pleased with myself for completing an entire suit, dress shirt and scarf. I always would laugh when future seasons would have to design menswear and they could barely make a shirt collar. While I knew my suit might have had some problems because of the fabric I chose, I was surprised to have been eliminated for it. Especially since there was a certain designer that literally safety-pinned and taped their garment together. But alas, *Project Runway* is not a "Best Sewer" competition and it's about the design. So while I enjoyed the actual challenge, and had a blast modeling for Chloe, this fateful episode ended my time on the show.

The other challenge that I dreaded was titled "Flower Power" and I suppose would have been considered our "Unconventional Challenge." We were tasked with creating a look for a Garden Party that was completely made out of flowers and plants. Ever since I could remember, I was never one of those children in school that could make some fabulous creation out of glue, glitter and old scraps of paper. This was not my forte. I would be the one drawing girls in big Princess gowns in the back of the classroom. When this challenge of making a fabulous look out of flowers and plants was in front of me, I had no idea what to do. To add insult to injury, we were given a budget of $100. In Manhattan, you can barely even buy a wilting grocery store bouquet for that price. I recall buying mainly plants (because they were cheap), laying them on my work table at Parsons, and spraying them with water for what seemed like hours. I was stalling since I could not come up with a single idea. When they talk about being paralyzed by fear, this was exactly the definition of my state of mind. I finally did come up with a concept and was happy that I just completed the design. The most annoying part of the judging wasn't that they didn't love my design, but that they continually wanted to see more flowers on ALL our dresses. All I wanted to do was scream and say "DO YOU KNOW THE PRICE OF FLOWERS IN NY?!"

# Favorite Judge

The ever-fabulous Diane von Furstenberg was my favorite judge from Season 2. Style icon von Furstenberg judged our second challenge, which was to design an outfit using our own clothes. She was also our first guest judge. I remember pinching myself as I sat across the runway looking at THE Diane von Furstenberg thinking how amazing and lucky I was to be there. She was every bit a Diva—and in the good sense of the word—as you can imagine. I think everyone in the room, including the crew, were on their best behavior. Everyone sat up just a little bit straighter in her presence and above all else, she was very nice and offered honest and constructive advice.

# Judging the Auditions

It could be argued that *Project Runway* really became a popular hit show during Season 2. As I alluded to previously, Season 1 had not really been watched by many people until the very end of the season and the president of Bravo really had to fight to keep the show on the air. But with the momentum of Season 1 and success of Season 2, the guarantee of a third season was inevitable. Soon, the production company and network began the process of producing the next season and I was honored to be part of the audition process in both Chicago and Los Angeles. As a designer, a former contestant and Instructor of Fashion Design, I assumed the position quite seamlessly and was happy to be part of the casting process for 12 seasons. At most all of these auditions, I sat beside Tim Gunn and a fashion editor from *Elle* magazine or *Marie Claire*. The days of castings were long and sometimes tedious but it was rewarding to be part of that pre-show process. I always looked forward to seeing if any of the designers we selected in our casting would actually make it onto the show.

As a judge, I tried carefully to wear three hats: "Instructor Nick," "Designer Nick," and "Contestant Nick" who had been through the process. I was always vigilant to defer to Tim as having the final word. I learned a lot from sitting next to Tim Gunn, during all those years. He was funny, erudite and very tough. One of the most memorable takeaways from judging the castings with Tim was the way he would tell someone who was young and had little experience that they weren't ready for *Project Runway*. Gunn would say "You are not fully baked yet... you need more incubating time in the fashion oven." I would have probably said "Go and work for a fashion company and then come back and see us!" But leave it to Tim to say the same thing but more descriptively.

During my years in the casting process, I did see a change in who applied and their reasons for wanting to be on the show. First and foremost, in the early seasons, the casting method was pretty much open to anyone who had garments to show and filled out an application. We saw an abundance of moms who had made their daughter's cheetah-printed cheerleading costumes and felt they could be on *Project Runway*. It was always sad to see Tim give them the heave-ho. But he had to, bless his heart. The casting process has changed now and candidates are pre-screened so instead of seeing hundreds upon hundreds, we now see 25 in a day. Fewer kooky designers bringing in their designs for dolls and pets, unfortunately AND fortunately!

At the same time, in those early seasons, there were tons of talented designers who had already achieved a level of success, but were looking to make it to the next level. I remember always being taken aback—especially when I judged in my hometown of Los Angeles—at the high level of talent. This was exciting to see, but it made me feel slightly awkward to be sitting there critiquing and judging fellow designers I had known for years. Almost always, I would either be "Switzerland" and try and remain neutral or let everyone know that I knew the designer and was familiar with their incredible work. This was never more apparent than when Rami Kashou showed up at the casting. He was an enormous talent that was very well known in the Los Angeles design community and the minute I saw him walk in the door, I knew that he was destined to be a finalist. Unfortunately for poor Rami, he happened to be paired in a season with a young designer named Christian Siriano, who as we all know now was destined for greatness.

## Guest Judging on Season 6

In 2008, *Project Runway* changed networks from Bravo to Lifetime. Season 6 would be the first season to air on that network. The show changed its location, leaving NYC for sunny Los Angeles and replacing Parsons with my alma mater, the Fashion Institute of Design & Merchandising, as the site of the designer's workroom. During the season's filming, I received an incredible call and request from the producers of the show: Would I be able to Guest Judge one of the episodes? It took me all of about 1.2 seconds to answer a resounding

YES! Only afterward did I double-check if I was actually available on the date and thank goodness, I was!

I could not believe my luck and was beyond thrilled by the invitation. Designer and judge Michael Kors—who at the time was still on the show—had been flying back and forth for his judging duties but for this one time, he was unable to make it. Therefore, they asked me to sit in his chair. My giddy excitement turned into outright nervousness when I found out I would be seated in between Miss Nina Garcia and Heidi Klum with the gorgeous and talented actress Kerry Washington serving as special Guest Judge. The sight of Heidi's smiling face instantly made me feel much better and as nervous as I was, it was a heck of a lot better than standing on that stage being judged. Season 6 was filled with strong women contestants and even from judging just one episode, I knew that Irina Shabayeva, Althea Harper and Carol Hannah were the ones to beat. Irina won the challenge and eventually won the entire season, while all three have gone on to do amazing things. I was humbled by the experience and grateful to have been asked to be part of such an illustrious judging panel. It felt like the ultimate feather in my *Project Runway* cap.

## Post Runway

During the years following my stint on Season 2, a lot has occurred in my life and my career. Being part of the *Project Runway* brand has been very rewarding for me and I consider myself lucky and fortunate for every opportunity that has come my way as a result of the show. I made sure to answer every phone call, respond to every email and do just about anything that the producers and the network asked of me.

Many months after my season of *Project Runway* aired, I remember Bravo's director of public relations telling me how she would get requests for interviews and appearances for specific designers from the show. For whatever reason, those offers would often be declined and so, she would then turn to me. I, of course, would do them all! Finally, it got to a point where she would just pitch me as the go-to cast member. She knew that not only would I say "yes," but I would be professional and do what was asked of me. I am very grateful for those times and having an early "cheerleader" on my side.

Thank you Sasha Cohen! Nick and David at the 2006 Winter Olympics
in Torino, Italy

I was just so humbled and excited that anyone wanted me for
anything and took advantage of everything which then opened many
other doors. You definitely can't just sit at home thinking that the
phone will ring or emails will come in and by the sheer fact that you
are on TV, you will be a success. It doesn't work like that; even if you
win the show. You have to work for it and go out and seek it . . . in
essence I was still . . . Getting the Coffee.

One of the biggest highlights that followed my time on *Project
Runway* was when NBC/Universal invited me to Torino, Italy to
cover the 2006 Winter Olympics and talk about the figure skating
costumes. I think this might have had something to do with my
obsessive excitement during the "On Thin Ice" episode! I was
overjoyed, and my partner David could not have been happier. Not
only was it my very first experience as an "On-Air" TV Commentator,

but I was also able to meet American figure skating royalty and TV analyst Dick Button. While we weren't allowed to stay in the arena after my commentary (security was tight and we weren't high-profile enough to score a ticket) David and I did get to attend the 2006 Winter Olympics Closing Ceremonies which in itself was truly, a once-in-a-lifetime opportunity.

After that first experience commentating at the Olympics, I have been excited to continue to work on-camera and have had a blast reporting on fashion for E! and TV Guide at the Academy Awards, Golden Globes, Emmy Awards and Grammys. I loved doing those shows because it not only gave me a venue to hand out my critiques and observations, but also a chance to teach the viewers about Red Carpet fashion, Haute Couture and everything in between.

The other TV appearance that I am constantly asked about is when I was on MTV's *The Hills*. I taught one of its stars, Lauren Conrad. To this day, almost everyone who recognizes me on the street or at an airport, always mentions how they loved seeing me on *The Hills*. These same people always ask me if I really did teach Lauren Conrad or if she was actually in my class. The answer to both questions, is yes and yes. She was a student in one of my Technical Sketching classes at FIDM. Subsequently, I even ended up having another *The Hills* alumni in one of my classes, Stephanie Pratt.

# Project Runway: Under The Gunn

Before I got the call to be on a new show called *Under The Gunn*, I had been asked several times to be part of another spin-off called *Project Runway: All-Stars*. In case you are unfamiliar, it is the same show as *Project Runway*, but with former contestants returning for another chance to win some money and various prizes. Every year I was called and respectfully declined.

Something about going back after almost ten years and competing again on *Project Runway* just did not seem right for me. Lots of the past contestants do it and good for them. I recall how wonderfully naïve I was back in 2005 when I did my season and that was a good thing. A lot has changed since then and I have become older and wiser. As much as I loved doing *Project Runway*, I was a little dubious of going through it all over again, especially the making-a-dress-in-8-hours-while-getting-no-sleep part.

Then came the call to be part of *Under The Gunn*. The premise of the show, as it was explained to me, was "The Voice but with fashion." The show was being hosted by Tim Gunn and it would be just like *Project Runway* with more than a dozen designers vying for the top prize. The twist was that instead of Tim Gunn mentoring the contestants, three former *Project Runway* designers would be taking over that task. Each mentor would get a group of designers and guide them until the final designer and mentor were crowned the winners.

The show's producers asked me if I could be one of those three mentors and I was intrigued. I liked the premise of the show and I was especially attracted by the fact that I would be mentoring as opposed to back in the workroom trying to sew a gown as the cameras got every second of the stressed-out process. I also liked the fact that the show was being filmed at FIDM in Los Angeles and that, as a mentor, I would have the luxury of going home every night, as opposed to the designers being sequestered just like the original *Project Runway*.

After much consideration—and a call from Tim—I decided to do it. I thought this would be a perfect venue to use my Fashion Designer/Fashion Business Owner/Instructor experience and put it to work to hopefully help an up-and-coming fashion star fulfill their greatest potential. I came into the show thinking that all those "hats" of mine would be a benefit and this would be easy. It wasn't. I struggled to find the "proper" way of mentoring that wasn't too hands-on or too "Instructor-y." I assumed my experience of patternmaking and comprehensive knowledge of draping and sewing would also be an added bonus. They weren't. I forgot that as a mentor on *Project Runway*, Tim Gunn never helped a designer make a pattern or suggest better ways to drape a garment. During filming, Tim pulled me aside and told me a story. He explained that during the first season of *Project Runway* a designer asked him to help thread the sewing machine. Tim obligingly sat down and threaded the machine. When he finished and walked off set, a producer approached Tim and said, "If you thread one designer's sewing machine are you willing to thread ALL their machines for the entire season?!" Tim had a "light bulb moment" and seeing my trajectory as a mentor, he was kind enough to share that humbling experience with me in hopes that I too could have an epiphany.

Thanks in part to Tim Gunn, who insisted I should be more "Socratic," I realized my shortcomings in my mentoring technique and eventually went on to help the winning designer, the fabulous Oscar Lopez, win the show and in turn I achieved the title of Winning Mentor on *Under the Gunn*.

Speaking of winning . . . the prize for being the winning mentor on *Under The Gunn*, as announced by Tim, included "A 2014 Lexus CT200h, a fashion spread in *Marie Claire* magazine and a spot as guest editor for one year." Now, let me rewind a little bit: When I was first contacted to be part of the show, neither Tim Gunn, nor any of the producers, mentioned any prizes. This, I venture to guess, was because they hadn't secured the sponsorships. To be quite honest, I never really cared about winning any prizes when I was on the show. I would hear Tim mention the prize package almost every episode and almost tune him out. My one and only focus was on helping one of my designers win the show.

When Tim declared that Oscar Lopez was the winner and therefore I had also won, Tim triumphantly announced that we would each be receiving a brand new Lexus. In fact, right after winning, they filmed us getting our keys from a Lexus executive (this scene would later be edited out of the final episode). Like I previously said, I really had not concerned myself with the prizes, until suddenly I realized that the day we were filming the final episode was David's birthday. I called him immediately and gave him the outstanding news that I was the winning mentor and that I was going to give him a fabulous birthday gift: A brand new Lexus!

About a week later, I received a phone call: I was informed that Lexus had "changed their mind" and that they did not want to give us a car. Instead of receiving the cars outright, the Lexus executives decided that it would only be a one year lease and that we had to get a $1 million insurance policy on the car. I couldn't believe what I was hearing, but at the same time I realized that one should pay closer attention when the prizes are described: "The Winning Mentor will RECEIVE a Brand New Car." It certainly didn't say that I would be the owner of a Lexus and not just a lessee.

Captain Benefit! Nick Verreos in the Under The Gunn Benefit Cosmetics Lounge

Needless to say, after pausing for about two seconds, I respectfully declined. I think I was both in shock and awe. The most disappointing part was that I had to tell my darling David that his birthday gift was not ever going to be in our garage. Oh, and in case you're wondering, I didn't receive the fashion spread in *Marie Claire* magazine or the one year guest editor position either. I would be lying if I said that this didn't leave a bad taste in my mouth, especially since it was the final experience I had with *Under The Gunn*.

But with bad comes good: While the show was airing, I received word that the makeup sponsor, San Francisco-based Benefit Cosmetics, had loved my participation on the program and wanted to work with me for future marketing projects. I could not be more elated to do so! Benefit is an amazing company and I had a fabulous time doing various appearances and events for them. In the end, this wasn't a prize Tim Gunn had announced on the show, but it was a great reward and I was thrilled to be able to turn lemons into lemonade.

# CHAPTER 10

## Threads of Advice

As a little boy growing up in Caracas, Venezuela and drawing my mom attending embassy parties, I would have never imagined what my life would be like all these years later. My biggest joy during childhood was the time I spent in my own "fantasy world." I am beyond grateful that somehow I have been able to live out my fantasy and carve out a career in this crazy industry. Not many people can say that and I realize that I am lucky. However, I cannot attribute luck to all the positive outcomes of my career in fashion.

Throughout this book, I have given anecdotes from my life and how I began having a "Passion for Fashion." I have tried to show how you can translate that passion into a worthwhile career and understand that mistakes and setbacks are what actually make you become a better designer.

Many people, young and old, always ask me if I have any advice for them to guide them in a career in fashion. In my years as a designer, there are several "threads" that have slowly "sewn" my path. I may have briefly touched upon some of these "Nick Tips" throughout this book, but I feel that they are worth emphasizing to aid you in becoming the best you can be. So, whether you are a future fashion student, a designer or are interested in working in the industry... take down these threads of advice. Hopefully they will be as helpful to you in your path to fashion fabulousness, as they were to me.

# Thread #1: No Should've Would've Could've... Just Do It

When opportunities come up in your life, even if they scare you to death, take a deep breath and dive in. While you never want to be reckless, grab ahold of every opportunity that presents itself and don't let fear stand in your way . . . Just Do It!!!

# Thread #2: Get the Coffee

While I do mean this literally, it also encompasses much more: Do everything! This is one of the most valuable pieces of advice I can give any young person thinking about a career in the fashion world—and I think this would relate to ANY and EVERY other industry. The people that succeed are the ones that will do every task asked of them and be proactive enough to ask for more. I always say "You are not a Diva, until you have a Diva resume." Until then, keep getting the coffee.

# Thread #3: Give 110%

One of the running threads in my life is to always try to give 110%. This advice has been very useful to me throughout my fashion life—from my days at FIDM to the present. Giving 110% has made me a standout, landed me many jobs as well as new clients, and has shown that I am willing to work hard and get the job done. I suggest you try it as well.

# Thread #4: Persevere

Julie Andrews once said "Perseverance is failing 19 times, and succeeding the 20th." Having the effort to achieve something, no matter what the difficulties, is an enviable trait and something that is not easy to do. There have been many times when I did not get the job, the order from a department store, the actress I wanted to wear my gown, or the TV hosting gig . . . I could go on and on. In fact, I used to say when God was giving out "Good Luck" tickets, I must have been at the bar! But I soon realized that often you make your own positive outcomes. If you cower and give up after every obstacle, you will never advance. My advice for anyone having difficulty in their life and career is to continue moving forward and persevere.

## Thread #5: Be Nice... But Not too Nice

Here is a newsflash that should not surprise anyone: The fashion industry is not always going to be a bowl full of Swarovski crystals. It can be immensely rewarding, crazy and even fun, but it can also be cruel. I am sure this applies to many other industries but it is particularly true of the fashion business. It is a cutthroat world and one should be ready for it. One of the many things I have learned is to be ready for the pretty and the ugly. While being nice and accommodating is always important, it is also essential that you do not let anyone take advantage of you. Be prepared to have a strong sense of will and passion for your work and not allow people to push you around. This takes time, and you might get trampled on before you learn this lesson, but understand that in this industry, you must stand up for yourself.

## Thread #6: Don't Personalize It

Several years ago, an unfortunate situation came up with a client. The entire project fell through and I continually blamed myself. I found reason after reason why the project failed because of something I did wrong. I was explaining my sob story to one of my favorite people, the Director of PR at FIDM, Shirley Wilson. She elegantly turned to me and without any dramatic fanfare, dispensed one of her Golden Rules: Do not personalize it. She followed up with a one sentence summary making a perfect case for why I should do as she says. And right then and there, I became a new man. I must admit, this is the piece of advice I have the hardest time adhering to, but every time I have an instance that I instinctively want to blame myself, I hear Shirley's wise words of wisdom in my ear. So, the next time you want to blame yourself for every problem in the universe; stop, step back and try and remove yourself from the situation. As another wise person once told me, "it's not always about *you!*"

# Thread #7: Know Your Fashion History

One thing that is so important, especially if you are embarking in a career in fashion, is to know your fashion history. Do your homework and study the designers that transformed the industry as we know it; from Charles Worth, Christian Dior, Yves Saint Laurent to Rei Kawakubo. Know why these people changed fashion and what their influence was on the industry. Learn your history early so when you begin working, you are armed and ready.

I like to give the analogy that a student of architecture, for example, knows the difference between neoclassicism and post-modernism. In the same line, you as a student of fashion, should know your fashion history—designers, style eras, and important influencers.

When your future boss asks you to design a Beene-like dress or a stylist says she wants her client to look like Bianca Jagger at Studio 54 in Halston, you should know EXACTLY what all of these references mean. If you do not, you might be sent to the "back of the fashion line." So, do not risk it: Knowing your fashion history, from A to Z, will empower and broaden your mind.

# Thread #8: Value Your Mentors

I have been lucky to have had several mentors in my life who have influenced me greatly. I didn't know that they were mentoring me at the time, I just thought they were doing their job and helping accomplish the task at hand. It was only many years later that I realized the impact and effect they had in feeding my "Passion for Fashion." Be open to opportunities to learn from your mentors. You might not always want to hear the advice at the time, but if you allow yourself to gain knowledge from their wisdom, you will soon realize the incredible value of the mentors in your life.

## Thread #9: Learn the Business

People often forget that fashion is a business. Why would you spend so many long years learning how to design beautiful clothing and then completely ignore half of the industry? The two parts of the business go hand in hand; you cannot have one without the other. So, while the business of fashion might often be complicated, tedious and some may argue boring, it is necessary. Force yourself to learn it. Trust me, you'll be glad you did.

## Thread #10: Be Passionate

Be passionate! Have excitement for what you do and for life in general. Your passion can be infectious and not only motivate you, but also everyone around you. The fashion industry can be a difficult and maddening business, but if you have the enthusiasm, no obstacle is too big. I, honestly, can't imagine doing anything else, and if you are like me and have a passion for fashion, share it with the world and you will reap the rewards.

# Acknowledgments

I'd like to thank, first and foremost, my design, business and—most importantly—life partner David Paul, for being my rock. Every time I introduce him to someone, I jokingly say that he is "my better half" and it is true. He has been my No. 1 cheerleader, my No. 1 critic and my No. 1 sounding board . . . my No. 1 EVERYTHING. I could not have written this book without his incredible help. Who needs a silly "Like" on Facebook or Instagram when I have David? He is that thumbs-up sign and much more to me. I have grown as a designer and a person because of him.

I would also like to acknowledge all the other "cheerleaders" who guided me in following my Passion for Fashion: You know who you are. But mostly, I'd like to thank my parents. What would I have done without my mom dressing up so fabulously on her way to a Caracas Country Club? How can I repay her for all of those sketch pads, Prismacolor crayons and *Vogue* magazines she secretly bought me? What would I do without my dad, who never judged me when I broke the news that his one and only son wanted to become . . . a FASHION DESIGNER! *Gracias, Efkharisto,* and THANK YOU.

# About the Authors

Nick Verreos grew up in Venezuela as the child of a Greek-American Diplomat father and a glamorous Panamanian mother. During these early years, he began his love affair with fashion, but always considered it more of a hobby instead of a potential career. After graduating from UCLA with a B.A. in Political Science, he eventually decided to pursue his true love: fashion. He graduated from the Fashion Institute of Design and Merchandising (FIDM) from the Advanced Fashion Design Program, and worked for 10 years in the fashion industry before launching his own clothing line, NIKOLAKI, in 2001. Celebrities such as Heidi Klum, Katy Perry, Carrie Underwood, and Beyonce have all worn his designs.

Nick received national and international attention after appearing on the hit TV show *Project Runway,* and more recently he was the Winning Mentor of *Project Runway: Under the Gunn.* As a TV personality, he has enjoyed great success as a red carpet fashion expert and correspondent for E! Entertainment, Style Network, NBC, and CNN International. Nick has been a regular panelist on TV Guide Network's Fashion Wrap for the Golden Globes, Grammys, SAG Awards, Primetime Emmys, as well as a live red carpet correspondent for the Academy Awards.

After teaching fashion design, draping, patternmaking, and fashion sketching for five years at his Alma Mater FIDM, Nick also became the official spokesperson for the college, traveling yearly to all campuses to inspire future students. In addition, he has reached over a million viewers with his popular YouTube show, *Design School with Nick Verreos,* as well as his popular style blog, NickVerreos.com.

Nick launched his NV Nick Verreos line of contemporary clothing in 2014. His collection has sold at Dillard's and Lord & Taylor department stores, EVINE Live shopping channel, as well as QVC UK, QVC Italy, and The Shopping Channel (Canada).

A native of Southern California, David Paul is truly a representative of the melting pot of American culture. Born to a Mexican-American mother, whose parents immigrated from Guadalajara and Hermosillo, and an architect father who hails from Louisiana, David spent his childhood growing up in sunny San Diego.

Heavily influenced by his artistic parents, David realized his own love of theater and the arts. He attended the University of California, Los Angeles/UCLA where he received his B.A. in Theater Arts, and subsequently, his Masters Degree in Costume Design.

Recognizing his interest in both fashion and costume, David went on to build an extensive resume in the world of entertainment and fashion styling. He has designed costumes and worked on shows such as *Queer Eye for the Straight Girl*, *Passions*, *Undressed*, and numerous other productions for MTV, ABC, FOX, and the WB.

David has also worked alongside Andre Leon Talley for *Vogue* magazine, and with such illustrious photographers as Arthur Elgort, Regan Cameron, Noe DeWitt, and Amanda DeCadanet, styling for Kate Hudson, Heidi Klum, Vanessa Paradis, Twiggy, and Heather Graham.

Along with partner Nick Verreos, David started the high-end clothing company, NIKOLAKI, in 2001. Their collections of upscale red carpet gowns and cocktail dresses have been worn by celebrities such as Beyoncé, Katy Perry, Heidi Klum, Eva Longoria, and Carrie Underwood. David is also the Creative Director for the NV Nick Verreos clothing line, which is available on major Home Shopping Networks including Evine Live (USA), QVC UK, QVC Italy, and The Shopping Channel (Canada).